Introduction to Shopping Centre Management & Leasing

M. Nauman Thakur

Copyright © 2024 by M. Nauman Thakur

All rights reserved.

This book or any portion thereof may not be reproduced or used in any manner whatsoever without the express written permission of the respective writer of the respective content except for the use of brief quotations in a book review.

The writer of the respective work holds sole responsibility for the originality of the content and The Write Order is not responsible in any way whatsoever.

Printed in India

ISBN: 978-93-6045-001-4

First Printing, 2024

The Write Order
A division of Nasadiya Technologies Private Ltd.
Koramangala, Bengaluru
Karnataka-560029

THE WRITE ORDER PUBLICATIONS.

www.thewriteorder.com

Edited by Pooja

Typeset by MAP Systems, Bengaluru

Book Cover designed by Sankhasubhro Nath

Publishing Consultant - Samyuktha Prasanan

Mama, until we meet again

Acknowledgement

I am immensely grateful for the support and encouragement I received while creating the "Handbook on Shopping Mall Management: Simplified". It would not have been possible without the invaluable contributions and inspiration of the following individuals and organisations:

1. ICSC/MECSC: Their initial guidance and expertise in the shopping centre management field provided the foundation for this handbook's content.

2. Samyuktha, Project Coordinator: For the unwavering support and belief in this project, encouraged me to bring this handbook to fruition.

3. My lovely wife, Dr Irum and my handsome sons Nooran and Naushan: Their invaluable feedback and constructive suggestions helped shape the content.

4. My adorable sisters Dr Nousheen, Dr Naushaba, Dr Natasha Thakur and Dr Arshi: For their constant support, motivation and encouragement kept me focused and inspired throughout the writing process.

I would also like to express my gratitude to all the shopping centre management professionals whose dedication and commitment to excellence continually push the industry forward. This handbook is dedicated to all of you, as you play a crucial role in shaping the vibrant world of shopping centres.

Above all, I extend my heartfelt thanks to my father, Mr. G.M. Thakur for believing in my capabilities, encouraging and always supportive during this journey.

Lastly, with your unwavering support, this handbook aims to empower and enhance the knowledge of professionals in the shopping centre management community.

M. Nauman Thakur
CEO and Founder
Bricks and Clicks
Mall Management & Retail Advisory Company

Preface

Welcome to the Handbook on Shopping Mall Management: Simplified, a comprehensive guide designed for professionals already immersed in the dynamic world of shopping centre management. This handbook is intended to serve as a valuable resource and reference, offering essential insights, strategies, and best practices to enhance your expertise and efficiency in running a successful shopping centre.

The shopping centre industry continues to evolve rapidly, demanding adaptable and knowledgeable professionals who can navigate the challenges and opportunities it presents. With this handbook, we aim to consolidate the core areas of shopping centre management into easily accessible modules that cover the essentials.

Feedback

As of now, the proposed chapters and modules cover the core aspects of shopping centre management, providing a solid foundation for professionals in this field. However, I encourage readers and users of this handbook to provide feedback and suggestions for improvement.

As the industry continues to evolve, we aim to update and expand this guide to ensure it remains a relevant and valuable resource for shopping centre management professionals.

I hope this handbook serves as an indispensable tool for daily shopping centre operations and decision-making, empowering to tackle challenges with confidence and ingenuity. May this book lead the readers towards even greater success and excellence in the vibrant world of shopping centre management.

Happy reading and best wishes for your continued success!

M Nauman Thakur
CEO and Founder
Bricks and Clicks
Mall Management & Retail Advisory Company

Contents

Acknowledgement	vii
Preface	ix
Feedback	xi

Module 1: Gateway To Leasing In Shopping Centre Management — 15
- Leasing In Shopping Centres — 15
- Importance Of Leasing — 15
- Key Players In The Leasing Process — 15
- Essential Core Elements In Leasing — 16
- Key Takeaways — 20
- Zoning Assessment — 21
- Mall Positioning — 21
- Key Takeaways — 21
- Leasing Terminology And Concepts — 27

Module 2: Tenant Mix And Merchandising Strategies — 29
- Tenant Mix And Merchandising Strategies — 29
- Defining Tenant Mix And Its Importance — 29
- Types Of Tenants And Their Roles — 29
- Leasing And Merchandising Strategies For Optimum Tenancy Mix — 30
- Leasing Plan — 30
- Key Takeaways — 35

Module 3: Lease Negotiation & Documentation Process   37
- Lease Negotiation Process   37

Module 4: Lease Administration And Tenant Relations   41

Module 5: Lease Renewals And Expansions   45

Module 6: Emerging Trends And Future Outlook   49
- Leasing Terms   53
- Questions And Answers Session - Leasing   55

Appendix   57
- Appendix 3 A   64
- Appendix 3 B   65

Glossary   77
- Leasing   77

1

Introduction to the Shopping Centres And Their Significance

Shopping centres play a vital role in the economy as they constitute a crucial component of the continually evolving retail industry. They encompass various types of retail establishments, including department stores, hypermarkets, speciality stores, food and beverage outlets, and entertainment venues.

These centres provide a physical platform for retailers, acting as a one-stop destination for shoppers and creating opportunities for businesses to connect with their target audience by offering a diverse range of goods and services.

The scale and impact of shopping centres on economic growth are substantial, with their contribution expected to skyrocket. It is projected that by the year 2030, the shopping centre industry will reach a staggering value of 30 trillion dollars, further solidifying its significance as a driver of overall economic expansion.

This paves the way for more economic activity, even in the smallest of communities. As such, the significance of shopping centres is even more amplified and highlighted. Stores of varying sizes find their way to shopping centres.

Whatever it is, shopping centres become a convenient venue for all the best finds without going far from home.

Advantages Of Shopping Centres Within The Community

One of the biggest advantages is the creation of employment opportunities. <u>Shopping centres provide jobs for people of all ages and backgrounds, from sales associates to security guards</u>. These jobs help to reduce unemployment rates in the area and contribute to the local economy by providing a source of income for the employees.

Secondly, they offer a diverse range of goods and services from Fashion Apparel, Cosmetics & Perfumes, Beauty Wellness lifestyle centres, F&B dinings, Speciality Stores like Toys, books & Electronics besides Home Decor. Shopping centres provide a one-stop shop for all your needs.

This not only saves time and money for consumers but also supports local businesses. Small businesses are often allowed to establish a presence in shopping centres alongside larger retailers, allowing them to reach a wider audience and increase their customer base. This contributes to the overall growth and development of the local economy.

Shopping Centre As A Community Hub

Shopping centres play an important role in communities by providing a central location for people to shop, socialise, and access services. They serve as a hub for local businesses, creating jobs and supporting the local economy.

Additionally, shopping centres are great community gathering places, hosting events and activities that bring people together. They can also serve as a convenient location for people to run errands and access a variety of goods and services all in one place, which can be particularly beneficial for people without access to a car or who have mobility limitations.

What Makes A Good Shopping Centre?

This is a question that many people ask when they are looking for a new place to shop. Many factors make them great, but some of the most important ones include the following:

1. **Location:** Location is one of the most important factors to consider. It should be easily accessible and close to other amenities such as public transport, restaurants, and cafes.

2. **Selection Of Stores:** A good centre should have a wide selection of stores that cater to different needs and tastes. There should be something for everyone, from fashion to home goods.

3. **Customer Service:** The staff should be friendly and provide assistance and advice when needed.

4. **Cleanliness:** A shopping centre should be clean and well-maintained. This includes the stores, the bathrooms, and the common areas.

5. **Safety:** The establishment should be safe for both customers and employees. There should be adequate security measures in place to deter crime and ensure the safety of everyone. These are just some of the factors that make a good shopping centre.

Q&A SESSION - SHOPPING CENTRES

Q1: What is the significance of shopping centres within the community?

1A: Shopping centres serve as community hubs by providing a central location for people to shop, socialise, and access various services. They contribute to the local economy, create job opportunities, and offer convenience and a wide range of products and services to the community.

Q2: What are the different types of shopping malls?

2A: Shopping centres can be categorised into various types, including regional malls, neighbourhood centres, power centres, lifestyle centres, outlet malls, and mixed-use developments. Each type caters to different consumer needs and preferences.

Introduction to Shopping Centre Management & Leasing

> **Q3: What makes a good shopping centre?**
>
> 3A: A good shopping centre typically exhibits qualities such as a desirable location, a diverse mix of retailers, a pleasant and inviting atmosphere, convenient amenities and services, adequate parking facilities, effective management and maintenance, and a focus on customer satisfaction.
>
> **Q4: What is leasing in the context of shopping centres?**
>
> 4A: Leasing in shopping centres refers to the process of renting out retail space to tenants or businesses. It involves negotiations, agreements, and the management of leasing operations within the shopping centre.

SHOPPING CENTRE MANAGEMENT

"The shopping centre industry is indeed a trillion-dollar industry, indicating its significant scale and economic impact. The success of the industry can be attributed to various factors such as consumer demand, retail growth, urbanisation, and changing consumer preferences. <u>The continuous development and expansion of shopping centres globally, along with their ability to attract a large number of customers, contribute to the industry's substantial revenue generation.</u>"

Keeping this in mind the career growth for Shopping Centre professionals globally and especially in India is high in demand and especially the role of a Shopping Centre Manager or Executive holds significant potential and importance, especially considering the growth and prominence of the shopping centre industry globally.

<u>Brief and overview of the significance of a career as a Shopping Centre Manager or Executive:</u>

A Shopping Centre Manager or Executive is responsible for overseeing the operations, management, and development of a shopping centre or mall. Their primary objective is to ensure the smooth functioning and success of the shopping centre while enhancing the overall shopping experience for visitors and maximising profitability for tenants.

The significance of a career in shopping centre management can be attributed to several factors:

Growing Industry

The shopping centre industry has experienced significant growth worldwide, driven by consumer demand, urbanisation, and changing retail trends. This growth has led to an increased need for skilled professionals who can effectively manage and optimise shopping centre operations.

Diverse Responsibilities

Shopping Centre Managers or Executives have diverse responsibilities, ranging from leasing and tenant management to marketing, facility maintenance, financial management, and customer experience enhancement. This breadth of responsibilities allows for continuous learning, development, and the opportunity to make a tangible impact on the success of the shopping centre.

Business and Financial Management

Shopping Centre Managers or Executives play a crucial role in driving financial performance and profitability. They are responsible for budgeting, cost control, revenue generation, lease negotiations, and maintaining positive relationships with tenants and stakeholders. Effective financial management skills are highly valued in this career path.

Customer Experience Focus

Creating a positive and enjoyable shopping experience is vital for the success of a shopping centre. Managers and Executives in this field have the opportunity to shape the overall ambiance, aesthetics, tenant mix, events, and amenities within the centre to attract and retain visitors. Enhancing customer satisfaction and loyalty is a key aspect of the role.

Dynamic and Collaborative Work Environment

Shopping centre management involves working with a diverse range of stakeholders, including tenants, vendors, contractors, and local authorities. Collaboration, problem-solving, and effective communication are essential skills in this career. Additionally, the dynamic nature of the industry ensures that no two days are the same, providing constant challenges and opportunities for growth.

In summary, a career as a Shopping Centre Manager or Executive offers significant opportunities due to the growth of the shopping centre industry globally. With diverse responsibilities, a focus on financial management, customer experience enhancement, and a collaborative work environment, professionals in this field can play a pivotal role in the success and profitability of shopping centres.

Shopping Centre Management is the process of overseeing and coordinating the various operations and services of a shopping centre to ensure its smooth and efficient functioning. It involves a wide range of responsibilities, including leasing, marketing, facility management (FM) operations, accounts, human resources (HR), and customer services.

Professional management is crucial for the successful operation of a shopping centre due to the complexities involved and the need to provide a positive experience for both tenants and shoppers. We will define each of these elements and highlight their importance, advantages, and the services they encompass.

Leasing

Leasing is a fundamental aspect of shopping centre management. It involves attracting and securing tenants to occupy retail spaces within the shopping centre. This process includes identifying potential tenants, negotiating lease agreements, managing lease renewals, and handling tenant relationships. Professional leasing management ensures a diverse tenant mix, optimal occupancy rates, and a consistent revenue stream for the shopping centre.

Marketing

Marketing plays a crucial role in attracting shoppers and promoting the shopping centre. It involves developing and implementing strategic marketing plans, advertising campaigns, and promotional events to increase footfall, create brand awareness, and drive sales. Effective marketing management enhances the shopping centre's reputation, increases tenant visibility, and contributes to the overall success of the retail businesses within the centre.

Facility Management (FM) Operations

Facility Management Operations encompass the day-to-day management and maintenance of the shopping centre's physical infrastructure and systems. This includes managing building maintenance, security, cleaning, parking facilities, landscaping, and utilities. Professional FM operations ensure a safe, clean, and well-functioning environment for shoppers, tenants, and employees, enhancing the overall shopping experience and protecting the shopping centre's assets.

Accounts

Accounting is a vital component of shopping centre management. It involves managing financial transactions, budgeting, financial reporting, and ensuring compliance with taxation and accounting regulations. Effective accounting management provides accurate financial information, facilitates strategic decision-making, and ensures the financial stability and profitability of the shopping centre.

Human Resources (HR)

Human Resources management focuses on the recruitment, training, development, and management of the shopping centre's employees. It includes hiring and onboarding staff, implementing HR policies and procedures, managing employee performance, and fostering a positive work environment. Professional HR management ensures a competent and motivated workforce, fosters tenant and customer satisfaction, and maintains high standards of service within the shopping centre.

Customer Services

Customer Services are a critical aspect of shopping centre management as they directly impact the satisfaction and loyalty of shoppers. It involves providing information, assistance, and resolving customer queries or complaints promptly and efficiently. Customer service management aims to create a welcoming and convenient shopping environment, foster positive customer experiences, and build long-term relationships with shoppers and tenants.

Professional shopping centre management offers several advantages

a) **Expertise and Experience:**

Professional management brings a wealth of expertise and experience in various areas of shopping centre operations. This knowledge helps in making informed decisions, implementing best practices, and optimising the performance of the shopping centre.

b) **Efficient Operations:**

With professional management, the shopping centre's operations are streamlined and well-coordinated. This leads to improved efficiency, reduced costs, and enhanced profitability.

c) **Tenant Satisfaction:**

Effective management ensures tenant satisfaction by providing a supportive environment, addressing their concerns, and maintaining a positive tenant-landlord relationship.

Satisfied tenants are more likely to stay long-term and contribute to the shopping centre's success.

d) **Enhanced Shopper Experience:**

Professional management focuses on creating a pleasant and convenient shopping experience for visitors. This includes maintaining high standards of cleanliness, safety, and customer service, which results in increased footfall and longer shopping durations.

e) **Market Adaptability:**

Professional management stays abreast of market trends, consumer preferences, and competition, allowing the shopping centre to adapt and evolve accordingly. This proactive approach helps in maintaining the centre's relevance and competitiveness in the retail industry.

In conclusion, shopping centre management encompasses various elements such as leasing, marketing, FM operations, accounts, HR, and customer services. Professional management in these areas is essential for the effective operation of a shopping centre, ensuring tenant satisfaction, enhancing the shopper experience, and driving financial success with expert management, a shopping centre can thrive in a competitive market and become a preferred destination for both tenants and shoppers.

Q & A SHOPPING CENTRE MANAGEMENT AND ITS ROLE

Q1: What is the role of leasing in shopping centre management?

A1: Leasing is crucial for attracting and securing tenants, negotiating lease agreements, and maintaining a diverse tenant mix, ensuring optimal occupancy rates and a consistent revenue stream for the shopping centre.

Q2: How does marketing contribute to the success of a shopping centre?

2A: Marketing plays a vital role in promoting the shopping centre, increasing footfall, creating brand awareness, and driving sales. It enhances the centre's reputation, tenant visibility, and overall success.

Q3: What does facility management operations entail in shopping centre management?

3A: Facility management operations involve managing the physical infrastructure and systems of the shopping centre, including building maintenance, security, cleaning, parking facilities, landscaping, and utilities.

Q4: Why is accounting important in shopping centre management?

4A: Accounting ensures proper financial management by handling transactions, budgeting, financial reporting, and compliance with regulations. It provides accurate financial information, facilitates decision-making, and ensures the financial stability of the shopping centre.

Q5: What is the role of human resources in shopping centre management?

5A: Human resources management focuses on the recruitment, training, development, and management of employees in the shopping centre. It ensures a competent and motivated workforce, tenant and customer satisfaction, and high service standards.

Q6: How does customer service management contribute to the success of a shopping centre?

6A: Customer service management aims to provide information, assistance, and prompt resolution of queries or complaints. It creates a welcoming and convenient shopping environment, fosters positive experiences, and builds long-term relationships with shoppers and tenants.

Q7: What are the advantages of professional shopping centre management?

7A: Professional management brings expertise, experience, and efficient coordination, leading to streamlined operations, reduced costs, tenant satisfaction, enhanced shopper experiences, and adaptability to market trends.

Q8: How does professional shopping centre management ensure success in a competitive market?

8A: Professional management stays updated on market trends, consumer preferences, and competition. This enables the shopping centre to adapt, evolve, and maintain its relevance and competitiveness, attracting tenants and shoppers alike.

Handbook On Shopping Centre Management: Leasing

Leasing plays a fundamental role in the operations of the shopping centre's leasing department and keeps professionals updated on emerging trends, changing consumer preferences, technological advancements, sustainability practices, and the future outlook for shopping centre leasing.

This knowledge enables professionals to adapt their leasing strategies, navigate the complexities of leasing processes, comply with legal requirements, build strong tenant relationships, and adapt to evolving market dynamics.

As a career advancement opportunity, it helps leasing professionals demonstrate a commitment to growth and expertise in shopping centre management. It enhances the credibility and marketability of individuals seeking career advancement in leasing roles. Employers often value candidates with specialised training and qualifications, and a leasing course can open doors to higher-level positions and increased responsibilities.

Module 1

Gateway To Leasing In Shopping Centre Management

Leasing In Shopping Centres

Leasing in shopping centres refers to the process of renting out commercial spaces to various businesses and retailers within a mall or shopping complex. **It plays a vital role in the overall management and success of a shopping centre.** Leasing involves establishing agreements between the shopping centre management and tenants, allowing the tenants to operate their businesses in the designated retail spaces within the mall.

Importance Of Leasing

The importance of leasing lies in its ability to attract and maintain a diverse mix of tenants, which enhances the overall appeal and profitability of the shopping centre. A well-designed leasing strategy ensures a vibrant tenant mix, maximises occupancy rates, and generates sustainable rental income.

Key Players in the Leasing Process

Key Players in the Leasing Process within the Shopping Centre Leasing Management:

This refers to the team responsible for overseeing and managing the overall operations of the shopping centre. They are in charge of leasing, tenant relations, and ensuring the smooth functioning of the facility.

Introduction to Shopping Centre Management & Leasing

1. Shopping Centre Manager

2. Leasing Manager

3. Leasing Coordinator

4. Leasing Executive

5. Leasing Admin. Document Controller

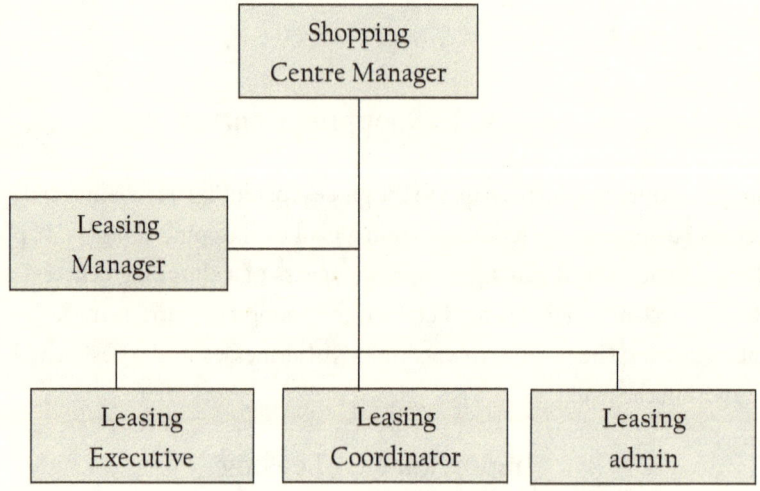

Essential Core Elements In Leasing

The pre-development stage of a shopping centre is a crucial phase that lays the groundwork for a successful retail destination. It involves several essential processes, including Demographic Analysis, Market research, Zoning assessment, and Mall Positioning.

These elements collectively guide developers in creating a thriving shopping centre that caters to the needs and preferences of its target market or Trade Area:

1. Demographic Analysis

The journey begins with Area demographics, where developers study the characteristics of the population in the trade area that the shopping centre aims to serve. This analysis includes factors such as population size, growth rate, age distribution, income levels, household size, and cultural diversity. Understanding the demographics helps developers tailor the shopping centre's offerings to match the preferences and demands of the local community.

Example: <u>In an area with a large population of young professionals and families, the shopping centre might prioritise trendy fashion stores, family-friendly eateries, and entertainment options.</u>

2. Market Research

Market research follows demographics analysis and involves a comprehensive study of the local and regional retail landscape. Developers assess existing retail competition, identify market gaps, analyse consumer behaviour, and consider economic factors and future growth potential. This research provides insights into the potential demand for the shopping centre and informs its positioning in the market.

Example: <u>Market research revealing a strong demand for sustainable products might inspire developers to emphasise eco-friendly merchandise in the shopping centre.</u>

<u>Marketing Research and Methods In Understanding The Trade Area Of The Development:</u>

1. Geographical Boundaries:

   The trade area is defined by geographic boundaries, typically drawn based on driving distances, commuting patterns, and customer behaviour. It can vary depending on the location and accessibility of the shopping centre. Commonly, trade areas are categorised into:

   - Primary,

   - Secondary, and

   - Tertiary zones based on proximity to the shopping centre.

Primary trade area from the shopping centre	0 – 5 KM
Secondary area from the shopping centre	5 – 10 KM
Tertiary area from the shopping centre	10 KM above

2. **Consumer Behaviour:**

   Studying consumer behaviour within the trade area provides insights into the shopping habits, spending patterns, and preferences of the local population. **This information helps in tailoring the tenant mix, marketing strategies, and overall shopping centre experience.**

3. **Competition Analysis:**

   Assessing the existing retail landscape in the trade area is crucial. Identifying competitors, **their strengths, weaknesses, and market share helps in positioning the shopping centre uniquely and identifying potential market gaps.**

4. **Traffic Patterns and Accessibility:**

   Understanding the flow of traffic and accessibility to the shopping centre is vital. **Analysing transportation routes, public transportation options, and ease of access from different parts of the trade area helps estimate potential footfall and customer reach.**

5. **Lifestyle and Psychographic Factors:**

   Consideration of lifestyle and psychographic factors, such as interests, values, and preferences of the local population, helps in tailoring the tenant mix and the overall shopping experience to resonate with the target market.

6. **Trade Area Mapping:**

   Geospatial tools and techniques are used to create trade area maps, illustrating the boundaries and demographics of the catchment area. Trade area mapping assists developers and retailers in visualising the potential customer base and making informed decisions.

7. **Survey and Market Research**:

Conducting surveys and market research within the trade area allows for direct feedback from potential customers. **Gathering opinions, preferences, and suggestions helps in fine-tuning the shopping centre's offerings.**

- **Customer Surveys**:

    Customer surveys involve directly engaging with potential shoppers within the trade area. Surveys can be conducted through face-to-face interactions, phone calls, or online questionnaires. They aim to collect information about customer preferences, shopping habits, brand awareness, and satisfaction levels. Customer surveys can also be used to gauge interest in specific products or services and identify areas for improvement.

- **Intercept Surveys**:

    Intercept surveys are conducted on-site, directly approaching customers while they are at or near the shopping centre.

    Researchers ask shoppers to participate in brief surveys, **capturing real-time feedback on their shopping experience and perceptions of the shopping centre.**

- **Online Surveys**:

    Online surveys are an efficient way to reach a broader audience within the trade area. **They can be distributed through email, social media, or website pop-ups.** Online surveys are versatile and can cover a wide range of topics, including demographics, shopping preferences, and feedback on the shopping centre's proposed features.

- **Focus Groups**:

    Focus groups bring together a small group of individuals representing the target market to participate in a facilitated discussion. This qualitative research method allows researchers to delve deeper into consumers' thoughts, opinions, and emotions related to shopping habits and preferences.

- **Observational Research:**

Observational research involves discreetly observing shoppers' behaviour within the shopping centre. Researchers can gather data on foot traffic patterns, popular areas, and customer interactions with stores and displays. This type of research provides insights into how shoppers navigate the space and interact with the environment.

- **Secondary Data Analysis:**

In addition to primary research, market research often includes analysing existing secondary data. This includes data from government agencies, market research firms, and other publicly available sources. Secondary data can provide valuable information about demographics, consumer spending patterns, and local economic trends within the trade area.

- **Competitor Analysis:**

Market research also involves conducting a thorough analysis of competitors within the trade area. Understanding the offerings, strengths, weaknesses, and customer perceptions of existing competitors helps in positioning the shopping centre strategically.

Key Takeaways

The Trade Area of a shopping centre refers to the geographical region or catchment area from which it draws its customers and where the majority of its consumers reside. Understanding the trade area is essential for developers and retailers because it provides valuable insights into the potential customer base and helps in tailoring the shopping centre's offerings to meet the needs and preferences of the local population.

Zoning Assessment

After demographic analysis and market research, developers undertake a zoning assessment. This involves examining the land's designated zones and **regulations to ensure it is suitable for commercial or mixed-use development. Zoning categories and classifies the type of development allowed, such as mass-market, bridge, or high-end, based on various intrinsic and extrinsic factors.**

Example: Zoning regulations may dictate the maximum building height, parking requirements, and other development restrictions that must be adhered to.

Mall Positioning

With demographic insights, market research, and zoning regulations in hand, developers proceed to define the mall positioning. **This step involves identifying the shopping centre's unique selling proposition (USP), choosing a theme or concept, curating an enticing tenant mix, devising a pricing strategy, and planning marketing efforts.**

Example: A shopping centre positioned as a high-end luxury mall might feature exclusive designer boutiques, upscale dining options, and premium services to attract affluent consumers seeking luxury experiences.

Key Takeaways

- The pre-leasing stage of a shopping centre is a critical phase that shapes its success.

- By conducting thorough demographics analysis, market research, zoning assessment, and mall positioning, developers can create a shopping centre that aligns with the needs and desires of the target market, complies with regulations, and stands out in a competitive market.

- This foundation sets the stage for the next steps in the development process, such as creating blueprints and engaging the leasing team.

CONFIDENTIAL LEASING OFFER LETTER

Ref: unit no.
Date:

To
Name of Tenant's Representative
Designation
Company Name
Address

Dear Mr./ Ms.
Sub: Offer to Lease Space in .... Mall

We are pleased to offer you a retail area in .... Mall, based on approved tenant mix, space, requirement and on initial Terms & Conditions as stated below:

Terms & Conditions:

Brand/ Concept	
Nature of Business	
Shop No.	
Approx. Area in Sq. Ft.	

Particulars	Year 1	Year 2	Year 3
Basic Rent per Sq. Ft. per annum			
Service Charges per Sq. Ft. per annum ...			
Water Charges per Sq. Ft. per annum			
Promotion & Marketing fees as per Contribution			
Total Rent per annum			
To be Paid (monthly/ quarterly/ half yearly/ yearly)			
Hand Over Date
Rent Commencement Date
Lease Terms
Fit-Out period			

Particulars	Year 1	Year 2	Year 3
Fit-Out charges	*** (as a one-time fee) current dated)		
Security Deposit	25% of the First Years Annual Rent (Current dated - refundable at the end of the Lease term less any applicable deductions)		
Booking Procedure	In order to book the premises, a non-refundable booking deposit (25% of the Annual Rent) is to be paid by the current dated cheque or inter-bank transfer		

Bank Details for transfer:	
Beneficiary Name	Name of the Company l Name of the Operator
Account Number	*******
Bank & Branch Name	Bank Name Branch Location TEL / FAX
Swift Code	
Payment Confirmation	Upon completing the above payment, please send us the scanned copy of the transfer voucher by email
Offer Validity	Subject to receiving your written confirmation of the above-stated terms and conditions by Date, otherwise the offer becomes non-binding
Notes:	

1. The final lease is subject to final approval from the Landlord.
2. The area of the unit is approximate and is subject to change upon confirmation of the final design.
3. All fit-out works are to be carried out by the Tenant, at its own cost including FCUs and hoarding.

4. The shop design and fit-outs would have to be approved by the Landlord's representative and have to be in accordance with the standards of the Tenant Manual.
5. All MEP works from the Landlord's end shall be terminated up to the lease line.
6. The tenant acknowledges the responsibility to obtain all relevant approvals, permits, licences, etc. from the local authorities.
7. Store completion to be in line with rent to commencement date ...... penalty per day to be changed for delayed stores.
8. Expiration of the lease and registration of municipality documents is solely the tenant's responsibility.
9. The above shall be read in conjunction with all the clauses pertaining to commercial and technical works of final documents.
10. Utilities such as Electricity and Water are to be paid by the tenants based on the actual metre reading.
11. A lease Agreement has to be executed to enforce the lease of the property and provide the details of the terms and conditions of the same.
12. Acceptance of this offer constitutes acknowledgement and agreement to the above terms.

Please note that this Offer Letter is not intended to create any legal rights or obligations. Rather, its purpose is to provide a summary of basic business terms. All of the legal rights and obligations of the parties will be set forth in a Lease Agreement which the Lessor agrees to provide to the Lessee within 10 days of the execution of this Letter of Intent. Furthermore, no such rights or obligations shall take effect until a lease document has been fully executed by both parties.

Please confirm acceptance of the above terms by return fax/email to enable us to issue a Lease Agreement and courier it to your office for signature along with the following documentation

Documents Required	1. Trade License Copy
	2. Passport Copy of Contract Signatory
Approved / Owner's Representative General Manager ABC Shopping Centre	Offer Accepted By Name Position Signature Date
Issuance Authority on behalf of the General Manager Leasing Manager	Witness

APPENDIX 1 -RETAIL APPLICATION FORM

1	Brand Name/ Concept:							

2	Franchise:		Yes		No			
	If Yes to the above question, please indicate the							
	country of origin:							
	(Also attach Franchisor information)							

3	Existing Store Location/s:							

4	Target Market							
	a. Age Group							

b. Price Points	Mass Market		Middle Market		Up Market	
c. Sex	Male		Female		Unisex	

5	Space Requirements:						
	a. Minimum			ft²	Maximum		ft²
	b. other requirements						

6	Contact Details:						
	a. Name of Applicants:						
	b. Company:						
	c. Address: PO Box			City		Country:	
	d. Telephone:					Fax:	
	e. Contact Person:						
	f. Designation:						
	g. Mobile:				Email:		

7	Comments/ Queries:						

8	Please attach the following documents along with this form (Tick appropriate)					
	a. Company profile				c. Product range	

b. Concept profile/ Brand profile			d. Customer profile			
e. Price point of merchandise						
Please note that the application will be considered INCOMPLETE without filling all the information and above attachments						
Signature:						Date:
Name:						

(Without prejudice, there is no obligation on the Landlord's part to accept this application)

Leasing Terminology and Concepts:

To effectively navigate the leasing process, it is important to understand key leasing terminology and concepts. This includes terms such as rentable area, common area maintenance (CAM) charges, tenant improvement allowances, lease term, rent escalations, and exclusivity clauses, which are explained below briefly:

- **Rentable Area**: Rentable area refers to the total square footage within a commercial property that is available for lease to tenants. It includes both the usable or occupiable space and a portion of the common areas, such as corridors, lobbies, stairways, and restrooms. The rentable area is the basis for calculating the rent and determining the tenant's proportionate share of common expenses.

- **Common Area Maintenance (CAM) Charges:** Common Area Maintenance charges, also known as CAM charges, are fees paid by tenants to cover the costs of maintaining and operating the common areas of a commercial property. These charges typically include expenses such as cleaning, landscaping, security, utilities, repairs, and management fees. CAM charges are divided among tenants based on their proportionate share of the rentable area and are usually paid in addition to the base rent.

- **Tenant Improvement Allowances:** Tenant improvement allowances are funds provided by the landlord to assist tenants in customising and renovating their leased space to meet their specific needs. The allowance amount is negotiated between the landlord and tenant and can be used for interior construction, fixtures, finishes, and other improvements. Tenant improvement allowances help attract tenants by reducing their upfront costs and enabling them to create a functional and attractive space.

- **Lease Term:** The lease term refers to the duration or length of time that a tenant has the right to occupy and use the leased premises. It is specified in the lease agreement and can vary depending on the agreement between the landlord and tenant. Lease terms can range from months to several years, and longer lease terms often provide greater stability for both parties. The lease term may also include options for renewal or extension.

- **Rent Escalations:** Rent escalations, also known as rent increases or rent bumps, refer to predetermined periodic increases in the rent amount over the lease term. These increases are typically specified in the lease agreement and can be based on factors such as inflation, market conditions, or a fixed percentage. Rent escalations allow landlords to adjust the rent to account for changes in expenses or market value over time.

- **Exclusivity Clauses:** Exclusivity clauses in leases grant tenants the exclusive right to operate a particular type of business or offer specific products or services within the leased property. These clauses prevent the landlord from leasing space to competing businesses or businesses that offer similar goods or services. Exclusivity clauses provide tenants with a competitive advantage and help protect their market share. Landlords may agree to exclusivity clauses to attract and retain desirable tenants and maintain a diverse tenant mix.

- Familiarising with these terms and concepts provides a solid foundation for engaging in lease negotiations and understanding the lease documentation.

- These terms play important roles in lease agreements and affect the rights and obligations of both landlords and tenants.

Module 2

Tenant Mix And Merchandising Strategies

Tenant Mix and Merchandising Strategies

Tenant mix refers to the combination of tenants within a shopping centre. It is crucial to create a balanced and complementary mix of tenants to attract a diverse customer base and maximise foot traffic. Different types of tenants, such as anchor tenants, specialty retailers, and service providers, play distinct roles in enhancing the overall tenant mix. Merchandising strategies involve clustering similar retailers, zoning specific areas for particular types of tenants, and selecting complementary tenants to create a cohesive and attractive shopping experience.

Defining Tenant Mix and Its Importance

Tenant mix refers to the selection and arrangement of tenants within a shopping centre. A well-planned tenant mix ensures a diverse and appealing range of businesses, products, and services, resulting in increased customer visits and sales. A carefully curated tenant mix enhances the overall shopping experience, differentiates the shopping centre from competitors, and contributes to its long-term success.

Types of Tenants and Their Roles

Shopping centres typically house different types of tenants, each serving a specific role in the tenant mix. Anchor tenants are large, well-known retailers that draw significant customer traffic and act as a magnet for other tenants. Specialty retailers offer niche products or services, adding uniqueness and variety to the shopping centre. Service providers include restaurants, banks, salons, and other businesses that offer essential services to enhance the overall shopping experience.

Leasing and Merchandising Strategies for Optimum Tenancy Mix

Leasing Strategies:

Leasing plays a crucial role in the success of a shopping centre, and one of the primary objectives of the leasing strategy is to position the shopping centre for achieving an optimal tenancy and merchandise mix for continuous and consistent growth. This involves keeping up with changing market dynamics and lifestyle shifts to meet the evolving needs of customers. By evaluating different generations and understanding their preferences and behaviours, leasing teams can anticipate the future customer base and customise the tenant mix and offerings accordingly.

Furthermore, these strategies aim to create a growth vehicle for retailers. By offering attractive leasing options, shopping malls can attract retailers who are looking to expand their portfolios. This not only ensures a healthy financial performance for the mall but also helps retain demand and spending potential within the community, reducing the leakage of customers to outside markets.

<u>Overall, effective leasing strategies require a proactive approach, market analysis, and a deep understanding of customer demographics and preferences. By anticipating future trends, collaborating with stakeholders, and creating a tenant mix that aligns with customer demands, shopping malls can position themselves for long-term success and growth.</u>

Leasing Plan

A leasing plan in the context of a shopping centre refers to a strategic document that outlines the approach and objectives for leasing the available commercial spaces within the centre. It is a comprehensive roadmap that guides the leasing process, tenant selection, and overall management of the tenant mix.

The objectives of a leasing plan for a shopping centre typically include:

- **Maximising Occupancy:** The leasing plan aims to achieve high occupancy rates by actively seeking tenants to fill vacant spaces. It outlines strategies to attract suitable retailers, service providers, and entertainment options that align with the target market and enhance the overall shopping experience.

- **Creating a Diverse Tenant Mix:** The leasing plan focuses on creating a well-balanced and diverse tenant mix within the shopping centre. It aims to offer a range of complementary retailers, ensuring that customers have a wide selection of products, services, and experiences. A diverse tenant mix increases foot traffic, encourages longer stays, and appeals to a broader customer base.

- **Meeting Customer Demand:**

  The leasing plan takes into consideration the preferences, needs, and demographics of the target market. It aims to understand customer demand and align the tenant mix accordingly. By offering desirable brands, convenient services, and engaging experiences, the shopping centre can attract and retain a loyal customer base.

- **Enhancing Tenant Performance:**

  The leasing plan focuses on selecting tenants that are a good fit for the shopping centre's positioning and target market. It aims to provide them with the right location, visibility, and support to succeed. By creating an environment conducive to their success, the leasing plan aims to enhance tenant performance, leading to higher sales and tenant satisfaction.

- **Long-Term Planning and Stability:**

  The leasing plan provides a strategic vision for the long-term development and growth of the shopping centre. It outlines expansion opportunities, tenant renewal strategies, and potential modifications to the tenant mix based on market trends and customer preferences. The plan aims to ensure the shopping centre's long-term stability, relevance, and adaptability in a changing retail landscape.

Overall, the leasing plan for a shopping centre serves as a guide to attract and retain tenants, optimise the tenant mix, meet customer demand, enhance tenant performance, and ensure the long-term success and profitability of the centre. It provides a structured approach to leasing that aligns with the overall objectives and positioning of the shopping centre.

Difference between Leasing Plan & Leasing Strategy:

I. **Leasing Strategy:** A leasing strategy is a broad and overarching approach that guides the overall leasing efforts of a shopping centre or real estate portfolio. It defines the high-level objectives, target market, positioning, and key principles that shape the leasing activities. The leasing strategy sets the direction for the leasing team and influences decisions related to tenant selection, lease terms, and tenant mix. It takes into account market conditions, competition, and the long-term vision for the property.

II. **Leasing Plan:** A leasing plan is a detailed and tactical document that operationalises the leasing strategy. It outlines specific actions, timelines, and targets to implement the leasing strategy effectively. The leasing plan focuses on the day-to-day leasing activities, tenant acquisition, and tenant management within a defined timeframe, usually for a specific property or a group of properties. It includes market analysis, target tenant profiles, prospecting strategies, marketing tactics, and performance metrics.

Age 0-5	The age categorisation of the shoppers within the trade area helps to understand the shopping pattern and spending, the detailed analytics give valuable insight into the shoppers visiting the Mall
Generation Z 5-22 yrs.	
Generation Y 23 - 34 yrs	
Generation X 35 - 53 yrs.	
Echo boomers' shoppers 54- 65 yrs.	

In summary, the leasing strategy provides the overall direction and guiding principles for leasing efforts, while the leasing plan translates the strategy into actionable steps and timelines. The strategy is more conceptual and long-term in nature, while the plan is more operational and focused on specific tactics and execution. The strategy informs the plan, and the plan ensures the implementation of the strategy practically and measurably.

Key Takeaways to Consider While Preparing the Leasing Plan:

1. **Current vacancy levels** – Review all of the leases on the property to understand the differences and risks between monthly tenants, vacating tenants, and existing vacancies. If you have several vacancies occurring close to each other, that can be a major weakness or potential risk toretail sales and turnover for nearby tenants.

2. **Upcoming Lease Expiry:**

   Any lease that is soon to expire should be resolved as quickly as possible, and preferably well in advance. That may mean the renegotiation of a lease with the current tenant, the relocation of a nearby tenant, the sourcing of a new tenant, or the expansion of one existing tenant into the same space. It is wise to consider a full tenancy review of the tenancy mix at least 12 months in advance in an ongoing way.

3. **Occupancy costs:**

   The costs of occupying premises within a shopping centre should be carefully considered and planned each year. Occupancy costs include rental, outgoings, and consumable costs such as energy, water, and gas. Those cost factors will impact the ability of any tenant to trade successfully in the future. Every retail property should be managed according to a budget of expenditure, thereby maintaining control over occupancy costs.

4. **Anchor tenants:**

   Anchor tenants, as major tenants in shopping centres, typically have lease agreements structured differently from those of specialty tenants. The size of their tenancy and the length of the lease necessitate unique terms and conditions. It is common for anchor tenants to have agreements that include step rents or a percentage of turnover and trade, in addition to a base rental. This arrangement allows the landlord to participate in the property's growth and the business success of the anchor tenant over time. As part of the agreement, anchor tenants regularly share their turnover figures with the landlord or property manager, and the lease includes provisions for a turnover rental.

5. **Reviewing Tenancy Mix:**

During the course of the lease progression, the shopping centre management should identify the non-performing tenants and need to relocate them from the existing ones to either improve their business or improve the circulation of their footprints prior to the expiration of the lease period.

6. **Turnover Figures:**

The leases for specialty tenants should be provided for reporting monthly sales. This allows the management to understand the business rationale, identify strong and weak retail trade in the mall, and take corrective steps as the case may be.

7. **Customer Requirements:**

Undertake regular surveys of the property at different times of the year; survey the customers and the tenants. That knowledge will help in creating a typical customer profile and, hence, a retail shopping strategy for the property. That retail strategy then helps in times of marketing and leasing vacancies.

8. **Levels of Retail Competition:**

Watch out for the newer retail properties that are soon to be opened locally. New properties can pull customers and sales from the shopping centre. Over time, that decline in sales can influence vacancy factors and new leases.

Market rents fall when vacancy factors rise. Incentives have to be provided to keep existing tenants, but those incentives come at a cost to the landlord.

9. **Existing Lease Documentation:**

The leases for a retail property should be matched to the intentions and investment requirements of the landlord. In each lease negotiation, it is then a simple matter of presenting the landlord's lease and negotiating with the tenant on any adjustments that may be required. It is easier to manage the performance of a retail property when you use a standard lease designed to meet the landlord's targets and intentions.

10. **Marketing plans:**

The shopping centre should have a definitive annual marketing plan with a systematic theme and flow of events and activations to more footprints to the precinct, resulting in more sales for the retailers and enhancing the value of the property.

Key Takeaways

The performance of the shopping centre is an ongoing and continuous process. Marketing plans should be set and analysed intermittently to be on top of the game plan to sustain and envisage the growth of the shopping centre targeting shoppers strategically and benchmark performance indicators well-tuned and aligned with the owner's expectations.

Module 3

Lease Negotiation & Documentation Process

Lease Negotiation Process

The lease negotiation process is a critical step in shopping mall management, where the shopping centre management team engages in discussions and agreements with potential tenants regarding the rental of retail spaces within the mall. This process involves several stages, starting with identifying potential tenants and prospecting, followed by initiating contact, conducting site visits, and finally, negotiating the lease terms and conditions. Effective lease negotiation plays a vital role in securing suitable tenants, establishing mutually beneficial agreements, and creating a thriving tenant mix within the shopping centre.

- Identifying Potential Tenants and Prospecting:

    Identifying potential tenants is an essential aspect of the lease negotiation process. Shopping centre management conducts market research and analysis to identify businesses that align with the shopping centre's target market and demographics. This involves studying market trends, consumer behaviour, and demand for specific retail categories. Prospecting techniques, such as networking, industry contacts, referrals, and attending trade shows, help in identifying potential tenants who may be interested in leasing space within the shopping centre.

- **Initiating Contact and Conducting Site Visits:**

    Once potential tenants are identified, the next step is to initiate contact and express interest in leasing opportunities. Shopping centre management may reach out to potential tenants through various communication channels, including phone calls, emails, or in-person meetings. The objective is to present the benefits of leasing in the shopping centre and to gauge the tenant's interest. Subsequently, site visits are arranged to showcase the available spaces and amenities, allowing potential tenants to envision their businesses within the shopping centre's environment.

- **Lease Negotiation Strategies and Tactics:**

    Lease negotiation strategies and tactics are employed to reach mutually beneficial lease agreements between the shopping centre management and potential tenants. Effective negotiation involves understanding the tenant's needs, motivations, and financial capabilities.

    It also includes determining lease terms and conditions, such as the lease duration, rental rates, common area maintenance charges, tenant improvement allowances, and any specific requirements or restrictions. Negotiation tactics may include establishing clear communication, active listening, problem-solving, and compromising to ensure a successful outcome.

- **Lease Documentation:**

    Once lease negotiations are concluded, lease documentation is prepared to formalise the agreement between the shopping centre management and the tenant. Lease documentation comprises a comprehensive contract that outlines the rights and obligations of both parties. It includes key components such as the lease term, rental payment details, security deposits, maintenance responsibilities, tenant improvement provisions, and any additional clauses or addenda specific to the agreement.

    Lease documentation serves as a legally binding document that protects the interests of both parties involved.

- **Key Components of a Lease Agreement:**

   A lease agreement consists of several key components that define the rights and responsibilities of the shopping centre management and the tenant. These components typically include the lease term, which specifies the duration of the lease agreement, the rental payment structure, including the base rent and any additional charges, security deposits; tenant improvement allowances; maintenance and repair obligations; rules and regulations governing the use of the premises; and provisions for lease renewal or termination. Understanding and including these key components in the lease agreement is crucial for ensuring clarity, legal compliance, and a smooth leasing relationship.

- **Lease Types and Structure:**

   Lease types and structures refer to the various arrangements and formats used in leasing agreements. Common lease types include gross leases, net leases, percentage leases, and graduated leases. Each lease type has its own characteristics and implications for both the shopping centre management and the tenant. The lease structure defines how rent and other costs are calculated and allocated between the parties. Understanding the different lease types and structures allows the shopping centre management to tailor the lease agreements to the specific needs of the shopping centre and its tenants.

- **Legal Considerations in Lease Documentation:**

   Lease documentation involves several legal considerations that must be taken into account to ensure compliance with local regulations, protect the rights of both parties and mitigate potential legal risks. Legal considerations include fair leasing practices, disclosure requirements, compliance with zoning and building codes, tenant rights and protections, and any specific laws or regulations related to the shopping centre industry. It is crucial to involve legal professionals experienced in lease documentation to review and provide guidance on the legal aspects of the lease agreements to minimise legal disputes and liabilities.

Module 4

Lease Administration And Tenant Relations

1. **Lease Administration Processes**

   Lease administration processes refer to the ongoing management and oversight of leases within a shopping mall. This involves various activities such as maintaining lease records, tracking lease expiration dates, monitoring lease compliance, and addressing any issues or disputes that may arise during the lease term.

   Lease administration processes ensure that all lease agreements are properly managed, documented, and adhered to, promoting transparency, accountability, and smooth operations within the shopping centre.

   - **Lease Compliance and Enforcement**

     Lease compliance and enforcement pertain to ensuring that tenants adhere to the terms and conditions outlined in their lease agreements. Shopping centre management is responsible for monitoring tenant compliance with lease obligations, such as timely rent payments, adherence to operating hours, maintenance of the leased premises, and compliance with rules and regulations. In case of lease violations or defaults, appropriate enforcement actions may be taken, which could include penalties, notices, or legal remedies, to ensure compliance with the lease terms.

- **Rent Collection and Financial Management:**

    Rent collection and financial management are crucial aspects of lease administration. This involves effectively collecting rent payments from tenants promptly and managing the financial aspects of the leasing process. Shopping centre management must establish efficient rent collection procedures, track and record rental income, allocate common area maintenance charges, manage expenses, and maintain accurate financial records. Effective financial management ensures the financial stability and profitability of the shopping centre.

- **Lease Renewals and Terminations:**

    Lease renewals and terminations refer to the processes involved when a lease term comes to an end. Shopping centre management must proactively identify lease expiration dates and engage in negotiations with tenants for lease renewals. This includes assessing the tenant's performance, discussing potential lease amendments, and reaching mutually agreeable terms for renewal. On the other hand, lease terminations may occur due to various reasons, such as non-renewal, mutual agreement, or lease violations. Shopping centre management must handle lease terminations per legal requirements and ensure a smooth transition for both parties involved.

2. **Building Strong Tenant Relations:**

    Building strong tenant relations is crucial for maintaining a positive and productive leasing environment within a shopping centre. This involves fostering open communication channels with tenants, understanding their needs and concerns, and proactively addressing any issues that may arise. Shopping centre management should establish effective tenant communication systems, provide timely responses to tenant inquiries and requests, and strive to build strong partnerships with tenants based on trust, respect, and collaboration.

- **Tenant Communication and Conflict Resolution:**

    Tenant communication and conflict resolution involve establishing effective channels of communication with tenants and proactively addressing any conflicts or disputes that may arise.

    Shopping centre management should promote transparent and open communication, providing tenants with regular updates, information, and guidelines. In case of conflicts or disagreements, a fair and efficient conflict resolution process should be in place, aiming to find mutually agreeable solutions and maintain positive tenant relationships.

- **Handling Tenant Requests and Complaints:**

    Handling tenant requests and complaints involves efficiently managing tenant inquiries, concerns, and complaints. Shopping centre management should establish clear procedures for receiving and addressing tenant requests, ensuring prompt responses and appropriate actions. This includes handling maintenance and repair requests, addressing operational issues, and providing necessary support to tenants to facilitate their business operations within the shopping centre.

- **Tenant Retention Strategies:**

    Tenant retention strategies aim to enhance tenant satisfaction and loyalty, reducing tenant turnover within the shopping centre. Shopping centre management should develop and implement strategies to create a supportive and engaging environment for tenants. This may include offering incentives for lease renewals, providing value-added services, organising tenant appreciation events, and fostering a sense of community among tenants. By focusing on tenant retention, shopping centre management can maintain a stable tenant mix and promote long-term success.

Module 5

Lease Renewals And Expansions

1. **Lease Renewal Process:**

   The lease renewal process involves managing and facilitating the extension of lease agreements with existing tenants. This includes identifying lease renewal opportunities, negotiating favourable terms, and preparing the necessary documentation. <u>The process typically begins well in advance of the lease expiration date to allow sufficient time for discussions and negotiations</u>. Shopping centre management needs to assess the tenant's performance, evaluate market conditions, and strategize on lease renewal objectives to ensure the continued occupancy of valuable tenants.

   - **Identifying Lease Renewal Opportunities:**

     Identifying lease renewal opportunities entails closely monitoring lease expiration dates and proactively engaging with tenants whose leases are nearing expiration. By maintaining a database of lease expiration dates and conducting regular lease analysis, shopping centre management can identify potential lease renewals and prioritise efforts accordingly. This involves assessing tenant performance, analysing market trends, and considering factors such as tenant satisfaction and long-term viability.

   - **Lease Renewal Negotiation Strategies:**

     Lease renewal negotiation strategies aim to secure favourable terms and conditions for both the shopping centre and the tenant. This may involve considering factors such as rental rates, lease duration, tenant improvements, operating expenses, and any necessary lease amendments. Negotiation strategies can include offering incentives to tenants, exploring win-win solutions, and leveraging market conditions to achieve mutually beneficial outcomes. Effective negotiation techniques can help maintain positive tenant relationships, minimise vacancies, and maximise the shopping centre's financial performance.

- **Lease Renewal Documentation and Amendments:**

   Lease renewal documentation involves preparing the necessary paperwork to formalise the lease extension. This includes drafting lease renewal agreements, outlining any negotiated changes or amendments, and obtaining the required signatures from both parties. It is crucial to accurately reflect the agreed-upon terms and conditions in the renewal documentation to avoid misunderstandings or disputes in the future. The documentation should clearly specify the lease duration, rental terms, any amendments or modifications, and other relevant provisions.

2. **Tenant Expansion and Upselling:**

   Tenant expansion and upselling refer to strategies aimed at maximising the leasing potential of existing tenants. This involves assessing the tenant's expansion potential, negotiating lease amendments to accommodate additional space requirements, and maximising rental revenue through upselling additional services or amenities. By identifying opportunities for tenant expansion within the shopping centre, management can increase occupancy levels, enhance tenant satisfaction, and generate additional rental income.

   - **Assessing Tenant Expansion Potential:**

      Assessing tenant expansion potential involves evaluating factors such as the tenant's business growth, market demand for their products or services, and their ability to support an expanded presence within the shopping centre. This assessment may include analysing sales performance, market trends, customer demographics, and the tenant's financial stability. By identifying tenants with growth potential, shopping centre management can proactively engage in discussions about expanding their leased space.

- **Negotiating Lease Amendments for Expansions:**

Negotiating lease amendments for expansions involves discussing and finalising the terms and conditions for the expanded space. This may include adjustments to rental rates, lease duration, common area maintenance charges, and any necessary modifications to the lease agreement. Effective negotiation strategies and clear communication are essential to ensuring a successful expansion process that benefits both the tenant and the shopping centre.

- **Maximising Revenue through Upselling:**

Maximising revenue through upselling involves offering additional services or amenities to tenants, increasing their leasing costs and contributing to the overall profitability of the shopping centre. This may include providing access to prime locations, offering premium signage or advertising opportunities, providing dedicated parking spaces, or granting exclusive rights for certain products or services. By identifying value-added offerings that meet tenant needs and preferences, shopping centre management can generate additional revenue streams.

Module 6

Emerging Trends And Future Outlook

1. **Evolving Trends in Shopping Centre Leasing:**

   The leasing landscape in shopping malls is constantly evolving, influenced by changing consumer behaviours and market dynamics. Some emerging trends include the rise of pop-up shops and short-term leasing.

   - Pop-up shops are temporary retail spaces that allow brands or entrepreneurs to showcase their products or services for a limited period of time.

   - Short-term leasing provides flexibility for both tenants and shopping centre management, enabling them to experiment with new concepts, introduce new brands, and create unique experiences for customers.

2. **E-commerce Integration and Omnichannel Strategies:**

   The integration of e-commerce and the adoption of omnichannel strategies have become essential for shopping malls to stay competitive in the digital age. This involves creating a seamless shopping experience across online and offline channels, leveraging technology to enhance customer engagement, and providing convenient options such as click-and-collect same-day delivery services. Shopping centres can also explore partnerships with online retailers or integrate technology-driven features within the physical retail environment to attract customers and drive foot traffic.

3. **Sustainable Leasing Practices:**

   Sustainable leasing practices focus on incorporating environmentally responsible and socially conscious approaches into the leasing process. This includes promoting energy efficiency, waste reduction, green building certifications, and supporting tenants with sustainable business practices.

   Shopping centre management can implement initiatives such as recycling programmes, promoting eco-friendly products, and collaborating with tenants to minimise their environmental impact. By adopting sustainable leasing practices, shopping centres can attract environmentally conscious tenants and appeal to consumers who prioritise sustainability.

4. **Future Outlook and Challenges:**

   - **Impact of Technology on Leasing:**

     Technology plays a significant role in shaping the leasing process in shopping centres. Advancements such as artificial intelligence, data analytics, virtual reality, and mobile applications have the potential to streamline leasing operations, improve tenant communication, and enhance the overall leasing experience. Shopping centre management needs to stay updated with technological advancements and adapt their leasing strategies to leverage the benefits offered by these technologies.

   - **Adapting to Changing Consumer Behaviours:**

     Consumer behaviours are continually evolving, driven by factors such as changing demographics, preferences, and lifestyles. Shopping centres need to adapt their leasing strategies to meet these changing consumer demands. This may involve integrating experiential elements, incorporating leisure and entertainment offerings, and curating tenant mixes and experiences that align with the evolving needs and expectations of the target market.

- **Addressing Environmental and Regulatory Challenges:**

  In India, shopping centres face specific environmental and regulatory challenges that need to be addressed in the leasing process. This includes complying with environmental regulations and waste management guidelines and ensuring adherence to local building codes and safety standards. Shopping centre management needs to navigate these challenges effectively and ensure compliance with applicable laws and regulations to maintain a sustainable and legally compliant leasing environment.

A) **Probable Leasing KPIs**

  1. To attain 95–100% occupancy by the end of Q4. The leasing plan should anticipate unforeseen challenges or circumstances, such as abrupt lease terminations.

  2. To retain the majority of the lease tenancy prior to lease renewals, we need to be specific on the number of leases expiring in the upcoming financial quarters (Q1, Q2, Q3, and Q4).

  3. To maximise the annual income projected through the leasing plan.

  4. To improve the tenant mix by increasing the overall percentage in fashion, entertainment, or F&B concepts, which would further enhance the value and income of the centre and tangibly increase the footprints.

  5. To be better prepared and equipped against the competitive malls and their challenges.

  6. To review and rework the internal processes and procedures for overall efficiency within the shopping centre management.

  7. To activate grey areas within the shopping centre, if any, which would transcend footprints in those areas and improve the look and feel of the shopping centre.

8. To increase the present leasable area for creating additional growth in revenue forecasted through the leasing and marketing plan.

9. Retrofitting and redeveloping the existing internal or façade fittings of the tenants after the lease expires to improve the overall imagery of the shopping centre.

10. Activating capital improvements within the shopping centre as per the master plan approvals without delay to be ahead of the competition.

B) **Leasing Appraisals:**

Further appraisals should be revised annually or biannually for every executive working in the leasing or, for that matter, the entire shopping centre management departments like marketing, finance, operations, HRD, customer services, etc., which would help the organisation achieve its goals and also improve the skillset of the workforce or executives. The appraisals are rated from 1 to 6, points, given below:

Sr. no	Items	1	2	3	4	5	6	Comments
1	Mall Occupancy							
2	Tenant Retention							
3	Efficiency							
3.1	Customer Database							
3.2	Competition Information							
3.3	New Entrants information							
3.4	Prospective Customers lead							
3.5	Visits							
3.6	Conversion of Leads							
3.7	Meeting Deadlines							
4	Revenue Generation							
4.1	Against Target							

Sr. no	Items	1	2	3	4	5	6	Comments
4.2	Cost of revenue generation							
5	Documentation							
5.1	Leasing Documentation completion							
6	Networking							
6.1	Job Knowledge							
6.2	Communication Skills written and oral							
6.3	Market Information							
6,4	Industry event participation							
7	Teamwork							
8	Leadership qualities							

QUESTIONS AND ANSWERS SESSION - LEASING

Q1: What factors should be considered in market research for shopping centre leasing?

A1: Factors to consider in market research for shopping centre leasing include demographics, psychographics, trade area analysis, and market trends.

Q2: What are some common leasing strategies employed in shopping centres?

A2: Common leasing strategies include anchor tenant leasing, mix optimisation, tenant clustering, and tenant diversification.

Q3: How are leasing Key Performance Indicators (KPIs) used to measure leasing success?

A3: Leasing KPIs, such as occupancy rates, tenant sales performance, lease renewal rates, and tenant satisfaction, are used to measure the effectiveness and profitability of leasing operations in a shopping centre.

Introduction to Shopping Centre Management & Leasing

Q4: What is the difference between gross leasing area and net leasing area?

A4: Gross leasing area refers to the total floor area within a shopping centre that is available for lease, including common areas, while net leasing area excludes the common areas and focuses solely on the leasable retail space.

Q5: How are leasing appraisals conducted in shopping centres?

A5: Leasing appraisals involve evaluating the financial performance, market demand, and tenant mix of a shopping centre to determine its value and potential for future leasing opportunities.

Q6: What is leasing in the context of shopping centres?

6A: Leasing in shopping centres refers to the process of renting out retail space to tenants or businesses. It involves negotiations, agreements, and the management of leasing operations within the shopping centre.

Q7: What are the key components of a leasing plan?

7A: A leasing plan includes various elements, such as market research and analysis, defining leasing objectives and strategies, determining rental rates, identifying potential tenants, creating leasing contracts, and monitoring leasing.

Q8: What are the key considerations in determining the ideal tenant mix for a shopping centre?

8A: The key considerations in determining the ideal tenant mix for a shopping centre include understanding the target market, selecting complementary tenants, ensuring tenant variety, balancing the retail mix, and assessing tenant quality.

Q9: How can shopping centres attract and retain high-quality tenants?

9A: Shopping centres can attract and retain high-quality tenants by developing a strong brand image, offering competitive leasing terms and incentives, providing attractive common areas and amenities, engaging in proactive marketing and promotions, and maintaining positive relationships with tenants.

Q10: What role does market research play in the leasing process?

10A: Market research plays a crucial role in the leasing process by providing insights on market demand and trends, competitive analysis, target market analysis, rental rates and lease terms, and feasibility studies for potential tenants or concepts.

Q11: How can leasing strategies be adapted to cater to changing consumer preferences and market trends?

11A: Leasing strategies can be adapted to cater to changing consumer preferences and market trends by offering flexibility in lease terms, embracing experiential retail, incorporating new concepts and trends, leveraging data and analytics, and fostering collaborations with innovative retailers.

Q12: What are some common challenges faced by shopping centre managers when it comes to leasing?

12A: Common challenges faced by shopping centre managers when it comes to leasing include finding the right tenant mix, negotiating lease terms, managing lease expirations and renewals, dealing with vacancies, and achieving desired rentals.

Appendix

CONFIDENTIAL LEASING OFFER LETTER

Ref: unit no.
Date:

To
Name of Tenant's Representative
Designation
Company Name
Address

Dear Mr./ Ms.
Sub: Offer to Lease Space in .... Mall
We are pleased to offer you a retail area in .... Mall, based on approved tenant mix, space, requirement and on initial Terms & Conditions as stated below:

Terms & Conditions:

Brand/ Concept	
Nature of Business	
Shop No.	
Approx. Area in Sq. Ft.	

Particulars	Year 1	Year 2	Year 3
Basic Rent per Sq. Ft. per annum			
Service Charges per Sq. Ft. per annum ...			
Water Charges per Sq. Ft. per annum			
Promotion & Marketing fees as per Contribution			
Total Rent per annum			

Particulars	Year 1	Year 2	Year 3
To be Paid (monthly/ quarterly/ half yearly/ yearly)			
Hand Over Date Rent Commencement Date Lease Terms Fit-Out period	_____ _____ _____ _____		
Fit-Out charges	*** (as a one-time fee) current dated)		
Security Deposit	25% of the First Years Annual Rent (Current dated - refundable at the end of the Lease term less any applicable deductions)		
Booking Procedure	In order to book the premises, a non-refundable booking deposit (25% of the Annual Rent) is to be paid by the current dated cheque or inter-bank transfer		

Bank Details for transfer:	
Beneficiary Name	Name of the Company l Name of the Operator
Account Number	*******
Bank & Branch Name	Bank Name Branch Location TEL / FAX
Swift Code	
Payment Confirmation	Upon completing the above payment, please send us the scanned copy of the transfer voucher by email
Offer Validity	Subject to receiving your written confirmation of the above-stated terms and conditions by Date, otherwise the offer becomes non-binding

Notes:

1. The final lease is subject to final approval from the Landlord.
2. The area of the unit is approximate and is subject to change upon confirmation of the final design.
3. All fit-out works are to be carried out by the Tenant, at its own cost including FCUs and hoarding.
4. The shop design and fit-outs would have to be approved by the Landlord's representative and have to be in accordance with the standards of the Tenant Manual.
5. All MEP works from the Landlord's end shall be terminated up to the lease line.
6. The tenant acknowledges the responsibility to obtain all relevant approvals, permits, licences, etc. from the local authorities.
7. Store completion to be in line with rent to commencement date ...... penalty per day to be changed for delayed stores.
8. Expiration of the lease and registration of municipality documents is solely the tenant's responsibility.
9. The above shall be read in conjunction with all the clauses pertaining to commercial and technical works of final documents.
10. Utilities such as Electricity and Water are to be paid by the tenants based on the actual metre reading.
11. A lease Agreement has to be executed to enforce the lease of the property and provide the details of the terms and conditions of the same.
12. Acceptance of this offer constitutes acknowledgement and agreement to the above terms.

Please note that this Offer Letter is not intended to create any legal rights or obligations. Rather, its purpose is to provide a summary of basic business terms. All of the legal rights and obligations of the parties will be set forth in a Lease Agreement which the Lessor agrees to provide to the Lessee within 10 days of the execution of this Letter of Intent. Furthermore, no such rights or obligations shall take effect until a lease document has been fully executed by both parties.

Please confirm acceptance of the above terms by return fax/email to enable us to issue a Lease Agreement and courier it to your office for signature along with the following documentation

Documents Required	1. Trade License Copy 2. Passport Copy of Contract Signatory
Approved / Owner's Representative General Manager ABC Shopping Centre	Offer Accepted By Name Position Signature Date
Issuance Authority on behalf of the General Manager Leasing Manager	Witness

APPENDIX 1 - RETAIL APPLICATION FORM

1	Brand Name/ Concept:						

2	Franchise:		Yes		No		
	If Yes to the above question, please indicate the						
	country of origin:						
	(Also attach Franchisor information)						

3	Existing Store Location/s:						

4	Target Market						
	a. Age Group						
	b. Price Points		Mass Market		Middle Market		Up Market
	c. Sex		Male		Female		Unisex

5	Space Requirements:						
	a. Minimum			ft^2	Maximum		ft^2
	b. other requirements						

6	Contact Details:						

a. Name of Applicants:							
b. Company:							
c. Address: PO Box			City		Country:		
d. Telephone:					Fax:		
e. Contact Person:							
f. Designation:							
g. Mobile:				Email:			

7	Comments/ Queries:							

8	Please attach the following documents along with this form (Tick appropriate)				
	a. Company profile			c. Product range	
	b. Concept profile/ Brand profile			d. Customer profile	
	e. Price point of merchandise				
	Please note that the application will be considered INCOMPLETE without filling all the information and above attachments				
	Signature:				Date:
	Name:				

(Without prejudice, there is no obligation on the Landlord's part to accept this application)

RETAIL APPLICATION CRITERIA		
General Information	Criteria to Summarise	Summary
Name of the Company	€ Local € International	
Footprint of Company	€ Franchise – Master or Sub € Number of Stores - International € Number of Stores – GCC € Head Office Location € Local Operator Name	
Financial Information	€ Established Company € SME € First Time Operator € Other Businesses € Independent or Company controlled budgets € Payment Controls	
Oman Setup	€ Stores already in operation € Registered Company € Local offices € Local supply chain € Retail experience € Staff availability € Government applications	
Category	€ Suitability € Availability € Price points € Adjacencies € Longevity	
Overall Suitability	€ Accept € Waitlist € Decline	
	AUTHORISED SIGNATORY	
Leasing Manager	General Manager	

APPENDIX 3 A

WAITLIST LETTER

Date:

To
Name of Person
Designation
Company Name
Address

Dear Mr./ Ms.

Further to your interest in leasing a space at ABC Mall, please note that your application was fully reviewed and assessed. However at this time we are not able to allocate suitable space for your esteemed concept due to space availability. In this regard your brand will be placed on our leasing wait list. Rest assured in the event of future availability we will be in touch should your brand meet the Malls requirements.

We would like to take this opportunity to thank you for your interest in our Mall and would like to wish you every success in your future endeavours.

Yours faithfully,

<Name>
Leasing Manager
ABC Mall
ABC Company

APPENDIX 3 B

APPLICATION DECLINE LETTER

Date:

To
Name of Person
Designation
Company Name
Address
Dear Mr./ Ms.

Further to your interest in leasing a space in our Mall, please note that your application was fully reviewed and assessed. However, we sincerely regret that we are not able to offer a space within the mall as the brand unfortunately does not meet with the mall's requirements at this time. If we have any openings in future that we deem suitable for your brand, we shall be in touch.

We would like to take this opportunity to thank you for your interest in ABC Mall and would like to wish you every success in your future endeavours.

Kind Regards,

<Name>
Leasing Manager
ABC Mall
ABC Company

I4

Opportunities for re-leasing space constantly arise, especially in larger centers. The purpose of this form is to keep track of lease expiration dates. Updated every six months, this report can provide the basis for planning your leasing strategy, long range as well as short range. This form can also be adapted to serve as a vacancy report for internal circulation.

Six-Month Leasing Strategy Report

Leasing Expiring within Next 24 Months

Space Number	Size	Dimensions	Present Tenant	Date Lease Expires

Grand Total   0.00   Average Rent per Sq. Ft.

Notes: Attach a shopping center floor leasing plan indicating the following
    A) Vacancies in RED
    B) Leases expiring within next 12 months in LIGHT GREEN
    C) Leases expiring within next 13 to 24 months in YELLOW
    D) Leases expiring with renewal options in BLUE

M. Nauman Thakur

Date _____

Rent Per Sq. Ft.	% Rent Per Sq. Ft.	Volume Year ____	Comments

#DIV/0!

Introduction to Shopping Centre Management & Leasing

E1	This form should be completed at the end of the year or prior to the policy's renewal, as a review of the previous year's losses. It provides the property manager with an indication of what risks to insure against or to increase insurance coverage of at the next policy renewal date.

General Loss Summary

Report Period: From___

Claim Location Code	Date of Loss/ Claim	Date Reported to Carrier	Type of Claim/Claimant	Location/ Description

Type of claim is either General Liability Bodily Injury (GLBI) or General Liability Property Damage (GLPD).

M. Nauman Thakur

_____to_____

Closed by Carrier	GLBI Paid/ Reserves	GLPD Paid/ Reserves	Other Paid/ Reserves	Expenses Paid/ Reserves	Litigation	Total Incurred
					☐	
					☐	
					☐	
					☐	
					☐	
					☐	
					☐	
					☐	
					☐	
					☐	
					☐	
					☐	
					☐	
					☐	
					☐	
					☐	
Total	$0.00	$0.00	$0.00	$0.00		$0.00

Introduction to Shopping Centre Management & Leasing

E6 | The inspection of leased and leasable premises should be completed semiannually to assure the proper standard of maintenance. This form will help you maintain insurance requirements according to the leasing agreement. It also highlights potential risk situations in unoccupied spaces.

Inspection of Leased and Leasable Premises

Property_____

Inspected By_____ Date_____

Time_____ Weather Condition_____

Area Inspected	Condition		Remarks
	Satisfactory	Unsatisfactory	
Building Interior			
Floors			
Tile			
Carpet			
Ceramic			
Other			
Ceilings			
Ceiling Lighting			
Fire Extinguishers			
Charges			
Missing			
Accessible			
Stairways			
Aisleway Clearances			
Electrical			
Breaker Box			
Conduits			
Excessive Extension Cords			
Connections to Fixtures			
Exit Lights			
Emergency Lights			
Elevators			
Plumbing			
HVAC			
Service Contract			
Storage Around			
Walls			
General Housekeeping			
Flammable Liquids Inside			
Stockrooms			
Well Arranged			
Clear Emergency Lighting			
Stock Height			

Page 1 of 3 E6 inspection of leased and leasable premises

M. Nauman Thakur

E3 — This form provides a list of those areas that should be considered when studying your insurance needs.

Insurance Program Checklist

Property Insurance
- [ ] Risks To Be Insured
  - [ ] Buildings
  - [ ] Business Interruption/Rental Income
  - [ ] Personal Property: Furniture, Fixtures, Equipment, Income
  - [ ] Data Processing Equipment
  - [ ] Property in Transit
  - [ ] Property of Others for Which You Are Responsible
  - [ ] Materials to be Used in Construction
  - [ ] Boiler and Machinery
  - [ ] Plate Glass

- [ ] Coverage Aspects
  - [ ] All Risk or Named Perils
  - [ ] Earthquake
  - [ ] Flood
  - [ ] Demolition; Increased Cost of Construction; Contingent Liability from Changes in Building Laws
  - [ ] Replacement Cost or Actual Cash Value
  - [ ] Coinsurance or Stipulated (Agreed) Amount
  - [ ] Deductibles
  - [ ] Course of Construction: Theft
  - [ ] Course of Construction: Resultant Damage from Faulty Workmanship and Error in Design
  - [ ] Rental Income: Actual Loss Sustained
  - [ ] Boiler, Machinery, Mechanical Breakdown

Liability Insurance
- [ ] Comprehensive General Liability
  - [ ] Limits/aggregates (each location)
  - [ ] Personal Injury Exclusions A & C
  - [ ] Broad Form Property Damage
  - [ ] Products and Completed Operations
  - [ ] Owners/Contractors Protective Liability
  - [ ] Blanket Contractual Liability
  - [ ] Owned/Non-Owned/Hired Automobile

Introduction to Shopping Centre Management & Leasing

E7 — This form helps the property manager distinguish the shopping center's insurance responsibilities with respect to each tenant's leasing agreement.

Lease Review Checklist

Insured _____   ☐ Landlord ☐ Tenant

Location _____   Area _____

Are insurance premiums part of common area charges?   ☐ Yes ☐ No

If a gross lease, does it provide for expense increase after a base year?   ☐ Yes ☐ No

Is there a 'Hold Harmless' clause?   ☐ Yes ☐ No

Does it cover the following situations?
- ☐ Negligence of Tenant
- ☐ Joint negligence of Tenant and Landlord
- ☐ Sole negligence of Landlord
- ☐ Not limited to insurance

Who owns tenants' improvements?   ☐ Landlord ☐ Tenant   If Tenant, does ownership convert to Landlord?   ☐ Yes ☐ No

Property Insurance Requirements

☐ Building
   - Who must carry insurance?   ☐ Landlord ☐ Tenant

   What Perils must be covered?
   - ☐ "All Risk"
   - ☐ Earthquake
   - ☐ Flood
   - ☐ Extended Coverage
   - ☐ Vandalism, Malicious Mischief

   Who pays premium?   ☐ Landlord ☐ Tenant

   Who is responsible for deductibles?   ☐ Landlord ☐ Tenant

   What is their financial obligation?   ☐ Replacement Cost ☐ Actual Cash Value

   Who is responsible for determining values?   ☐ Landlord ☐ Tenant

☐ Rental Value
   - Who must carry insurance?   ☐ Landlord ☐ Tenant
   - Are perils specified?   ☐ Yes ☐ No

M. Nauman Thakur

I3 | Completing a monthly leasing activity report is one way to keep a running check on the progress of all leasing activities. It is especially helpful for larger centers in which more than one leasing executive is responsible for leasing. A report such as this may be submitted to the development company's management as well as to all leasing executives.

Monthly Leasing Activity Report

_____
Date

Tenant	Date	Space No.	Comments
Leases--Requested			
Leases--Sent to Tenant			
Legal Negotiations			
Revised Leases to Tenant			
Leases Signed by Tenant			
Leases Fully Executed			
Notes:			

Submitted by _____

Page 1 of 2 (see file i3p2.xls)

G8	This form provides summary data relative to expense information as well as support schedules for each expense category, displaying the detailed accounts. This information is extremely important on a monthly basis, enabling a manager and investor to monitor the performance of the center in a timely fashion. Note the actual performance compared to budgeted performance is compared in terms of actual dollars as well as a percent variance. Operation modification can be made if necessary if this report is timely.

Income and Expense Statement

		Current	
Income	Actual	Budget	Actual Variance
Rental Income			
Minimum Rent			
Dept. Store Rent			
Percentage Rent			
Straight Line Rent			
Overage Rent			
Total Rental Income			
Tenant Charges			
Utilities Charge-backs			
Common Area Maintenance Recoveries			
Food Court Recoveries			
Real Estate Tax Recoveries			
Marketing Fund Revenues			
Insurance Recoveries			
Other Recoveries			
Total Tenant Charges			
Other Income			
Temporary License Fees			
Telephone/Locker			
Miscellaneous			
Interest Income			
Lease Cancellation Income			

M. Nauman Thakur

	Year To Date				Annual Budget	Prior YTD Actual
% Variance	Actual	Budget	Actual Variance	% Variance		
#DIV/0!	-	-	-	#DIV/0!	-	-
#DIV/0!	-	-	-	#DIV/0!	-	-
#DIV/0!	-	-	-	#DIV/0!	-	-
#DIV/0!	-	-	-	#DIV/0!	-	-
#DIV/0!	-	-	-	#DIV/0!	-	-
#DIV/0!	-	-	-	#DIV/0!	-	-
#DIV/0!	-	-	-	#DIV/0!	-	-
#DIV/0!	-	-	-	#DIV/0!	-	-
#DIV/0!	-	-	-	#DIV/0!	-	-
#DIV/0!	-	-	-	#DIV/0!	-	-
#DIV/0!	-	-	-	#DIV/0!	-	-
#DIV/0!	-	-	-	#DIV/0!	-	-
#DIV/0!	-	-	-	#DIV/0!	-	-
#DIV/0!	-	-	-	#DIV/0!	-	-
#DIV/0!	-	-	-	#DIV/0!	-	-
#DIV/0!	-	-	-	#DIV/0!	-	-
#DIV/0!	-	-	-	#DIV/0!	-	-
#DIV/0!	-	-	-	#DIV/0!	-	-
#DIV/0!	-	-	-	#DIV/0!	-	-
#DIV/0!	-	-	-	#DIV/0!	-	-
#DIV/0!	-	-	-	#DIV/0!	-	-
#DIV/0!	-	-	-	#DIV/0!	-	-
#DIV/0!	-	-	-	#DIV/0!	-	-
#DIV/0!	-	-	-	#DIV/0!	-	-
#DIV/0!	-	-	-	#DIV/0!	-	-

3   G8 income and expense statement monthly

Glossary

Leasing

1. **Leasing**: The process of renting or granting the right to use a property, such as retail spaces, within a shopping centre to tenants, known as lessees, for a specified period, usually in exchange for rental payments.

2. **Tenant Mix**: The deliberate combination of various types of tenants, such as retail stores, restaurants, entertainment venues, and service providers, within a shopping centre to create a diverse and attractive offering for visitors.

3. **Market Analysis**: The systematic evaluation of market trends, consumer behavior, and competitor presence in a specific trade area to identify potential tenants, determine the optimal tenant mix, and enhance the shopping centre's overall performance.

4. **Lease Negotiation**: The process of engaging in discussions and agreements between the shopping centre management and potential tenants to establish the terms and conditions of the lease, including rental rates, lease duration, and responsibilities.

5. **Lease Documentation**: The formal legal agreements that outline the terms and conditions between the shopping centre management and the tenant, including rights, obligations, and responsibilities of both parties.

These definitions provide a foundational understanding of key terms and concepts used throughout the handbook, enabling professionals in shopping centre management to navigate the content effectively and make informed decisions.

6. **Lease:** A lease is defined as a contract between a lessor and a lessee for the hire of a specific period on payment of specified rentals.

7. **Lessor:** The parties who are the owners of the asset/equipment that allows it to be rented for a specific period of the agreed amount are termed rentals for a duration period.

8. **Lessee:** The party who acquires such rights to use the asset rightfully on payment for that defined.

9. **Lock-in Period:** The period of the agreement between the lessor and the lessee, in which neither of the parties can terminate the agreement.

10. **Tenant:** Any occupier occupying GLA in the developer's property adjoining the enclosed mall by signing the lease or agreed terms derived by the developer.

11. **Tenancy Mix:** Defined as a combination of business establishments occupying space in the shopping centre to form an assemblage that produces optimum sales, rents, and service to the community and the finances of the shopping centre venture (McCollum 1988).

12. **Measurement of the Leasing Space:** The gross leasable area of the shop within a shopping centre is measured from the centre of the common wall (shared with the other tenant) to the outside face of the external wall. The external wall can be a shop front, a window display, or just a flat wall.

13. **Rent:** Rent are what the tenant pays the property or shopping centre owner for using the space as per the terms and conditions of the lease agreement.

    The rentals are normally calculated monthly or annually, depending on the methodology of the ownership for that particular shopping centre or property.

    EXAMPLE: The most common method for calculating the Annual rents is:

    The calculation multiplies the rent per square foot of the given space area unit, for example,

Rent Calculation = (Usable sq. ft * usable sq. ft rate each month) + (Common area * the rate per month for this particular area):

Assuming that usable area stands at 100 sq. ft with a common area of 50 sq. ft if the rent is Rs 150 per sq. ft for the given area of the unit and Rs 50 per sq. ft for the common area every month, then the rent each month will be the following:

(100*150) +(50 *50) = Rs 17500 per month. Further, to calculate the annual rent, simply multiply by 12 equal months = 17500 *12 = 210,000.

This Handbook is designed to provide a helpful and informative overview of the topics covered. It is not intended to be a substitute for more extensive learning that can be achieved through attending ICSC educational programs and reading additional ICSC professional publications.

You Write. We Publish.

To publish your own book, contact us.

We publish poetry collections, short story collections, novellas and novels.

contact@thewriteorder.com

Instagram- thewriteorder

www.facebook.com/thewriteorder

Shopping Centre Management - Marketing

M. Nauman Thakur

Contents

Module 1: Shopping Centre Marketing 1
- Introduction To Shopping Centre Marketing 1
- Interpretation 3
    - I. Above the Line Marketing (ATL) 3
- Advantages of ATL Marketing 4
    - II. Below the Line Marketing (BTL) 5
    - III. Through the Line Marketing (TTL) 7

Module 2: Significance of Marketing Budget, Marketing Calendar
            And Marketing Plan 9
- Marketing Budget 9
- Marketing Calendar 16
- Annual Marketing Calendar - Example 17
- Marketing KPI'S 19

Module 3: Digital Marketing 23
- Inbound Marketing Versus Digital Marketing 24
- Importance of Digital Marketing 24
- B2B Versus B2C Digital Marketing 25
- Types of Digital Marketing 25
- Marketing Automation 31
- Increase Communication Channel With Customers 33
- Key Takeaways 35
- Key Performance Indicators (KPIS) In Digital Marketing 35
- Digital Marketing Challenges 36

Module 4: Customer Experience And Engagement — 37
- Understanding Shopper Behaviour — 38
- Creating Memorable Experiences — 39
- Customer Service Excellence — 39
- Loyalty Programs — 40
- Feedback And Surveys — 41
- Community Engagement — 40
- Tenant Support — 41

Module 5: Data-Driven Marketing And Performance Analysis — 43

Glossary — 49
- Marketing — 49

Module 1

Shopping Centre Marketing

Introduction to Shopping Centre Marketing

Marketing is the process of exploring, creating, and delivering value to meet the needs of a target market in terms of goods and services, potentially including the selection of a target audience.

Marketing is a process whereby it encompasses a diverse and extensive range of activities within the shopping centre industry. It is often defined as one or more of its many components, such as advertising, sales promotion, special events, media handlers, community and public relations, crisis management, loyalty gift cards, merchant relations, investor relations, leasing support, seasonal decor, customer service, virtual merchandising, and merchant associations.

The dynamics of the marketing medium vary from shopping centre to shopping centre, and demographics in each trade area will be different.

In all probability, if the marketing medium is properly utilised in time, the shopping centre will flourish and have a major impact on the revenue stream and value enhancement of the property.

Marketing in its early years was through the merchant association of the respective shopping centre. The team was chosen collectively within the pool of merchant associates from the shopping centre, and they had the autonomy to host activities and attractions that would bring in crowds in the form of shoppers. Activities like special characters, circuses, wild animals, and adaptations of zoos used to be the favourites in those old days.

Such associations thrived for a decade or so, and later enactment bills were passed in many tenant leases to enable a unified cooperative clause by the landlords, which would felicitate a common marketing fund from the merchants and encourage them to participate in the marketing engagement.

Decades later, with so many changes, the cost of the marketing expenses, viz. print and advertising, overshadowed and reached the point that it was not possible to continue as it drew backlash from the centre retailers as well as the corporate corroborators that the centre marketing grew out of favour for them. However, later in the 1990s, a common advertising fund came into place, and the centre marketing team utilised such funds for a number of expenses like salaries, rent, seasonal decor, market research, and public relations, in addition to advertising and promotions.

Additionally, the value of the centre is directly tied to the net operating income. For the centre, marketing has to contribute to achieving the net operating income, though marketing brings in large revenues from different paradoxical sources, like advertising rights, corporate funding, specialty marketing and leasing, branding services, digital advertising, netc., which brings in a sizable NOI.

In a shopping centre's marketing, it needs to be robust and proactive in driving sales, which in turn drives rents, through three key components:

- Driving sales growth to drive fixed minimum rental rates.

- Tenant retention (surety of income flow);

- Marketing the centre and its available space to key potential retailers.

- Types of Marketing:

    Marketing can be classified into three important driving indicators woven very intricately around:

    1. 'Above the Line' Marketing

2. 'Below the Line' Marketing

3. 'Through the Line' Marketing

Interpretation

Above the Line, or ATL Marketing, refers to generally untargeted, massive campaigns to raise brand awareness and reach more people; Below the Line, or BTL Marketing, refers to the much smaller and highly targeted world of ads, aimed at individuals and with easy-to-track returns on investment and a definitive audience; and finally, through the Line, uses both of these approaches to gain both widespread brand awareness and focused, targeted returns.

I. Above the Line Marketing (ATL)

"Newspapers, radio and television are still extremely popular"

ATL are marketing activities that are mostly used to build brand awareness and establish goodwill. They are widespread campaigns, largely untargeted, and undertaken at a general level. *A good example of an ATL marketing approach is a national, or even global, TV ad campaign where the same ad is shown across the country to people of all demographics. Instead of targeting the ad at specific people identified already as potential customers, the purpose of the ad is to broaden a brand's horizons, reaching more people and establishing themselves more clearly and with a clear image.*

Other examples include print media and radio broadcasts, which again reach a multitude of different people over a large area, thereby accessing a mass market of prospective customers.

- Examples of Above-the-Line Promotion

- Television

Television is one of the most popular forms of advertising. People watch TV because it's entertaining and informative. They are able to see what you do, where you live, and how much money you make. If you want to reach people, you must use above-the-line ads.

<u>Above-the-line advertisements are paid for by companies. This type of ad includes things like commercials, infomercials, public service announcements, and product placements. These types of ads cost more money, but they generate more interest in the brand.</u>

We can choose various advertisement handles to include within 'above-the-line' campaign, some examples:

–**Local ads:** These ads are usually placed on billboards, bus stops, etc. They're often seen near where people live.

–**National ads**: These ads are typically seen during prime time or late-night hours. They're usually seen on cable channels like CNN, Fox News, etc.

–**International ads:** These ads are seen on foreign networks like BBC World News, Al Jazeera English, etc.

- **Print Media**

    Print media includes newspapers or magazines. The main purpose of using print media is to reach a <u>large number</u> of people quickly. This method has been used for decades, however, nowadays more people are inclined to use the internet to access content online.

- **Radio**

    Radio advertising is one of the oldest and highly effective forms of advertising. Radio ads are generally good for consumer recall and a call to action. Moreover, they can be *targeted to local, national, and international exposure* of customers.

Advantages of ATL Marketing

- ATL is a good way to promote and build your brand, but it is difficult to measure the exact impact and return on investment. This is why it is more untargeted; the purpose is not to see a precise conversion rate but to make customers generally aware of your brand or product and increase your visibility.

II. Below the Line Marketing (BTL)

BTL, however, is used in the opposite way to ATL. Below the Line Marketing is aimed specifically at targeted individuals that have been identified as potential customers.

Popular BTL strategies include outdoor advertising, such as billboards and flyers; direct marketing, such as utilising email and social media; and sponsorship of events. The latter is particularly growing in popularity, as giving a memorable experience to your potential customers makes your brand in turn more memorable and people more disposed to it.

<u>Examples of Below the-Line Promotion</u>

- Direct Mail

    Direct mail marketing can be an excellent way to reach out to potential customers. It usually involves printing large quantities of material in bulk, addressing envelopes, and mailing them to people. This type of marketing is most often used by businesses that want to send promotional materials directly to consumers.

    For instance, older generations tend to prefer receiving physical items such as catalogues, flyers, and brochures which can be sent out via delivery services. This is why they are still popular among marketers as it allows them to reach particular demographic and customer segments whilst still being able to personalise their ad.

- Sponsorship

    Sponsorship helps to ensure that ads are seen by people who are their target consumers. It also allows brands to reach new audiences, improve their publicity and build their reputation.

- Trade shows and Exhibitions

    Direct mail campaigns are also great for promoting your business at trade shows because they allow you to reach out directly to potential customers who may be interested in attending the event. Offering key promotional messages, such as exclusive offers or other incentives for joining, will increase your conversion rate and attraction efficiency.

    However, today, <u>businesses aim to take advantage of email marketing and online advertisements that cost less and take less time than traditional methods such as direct mail.</u>

- Email Marketing

    Email is a very <u>effective way of communicating</u> with customers in today's *digitalised world*. In fact, it is one of the most cost-effective forms of marketing and it *costs* nothing to send out. We simply pay for each recipient's inbox, and since we know exactly how many recipients there are, we can calculate your return on investment (ROI).

    <u>The effectiveness of email marketing campaigns is easy to measure.</u> For example, we can use analytics software to track opens and clicks and compare those numbers against previous campaigns. If a campaign generates more traffic, we know that the audience is responding positively to the messages.

    In addition, there are plenty of marketing automation campaigns and free solutions out there like Mail Chimp and Constant Contact. These platforms allow us to set up automated emails and newsletters without having to do it yourself. They also provide templates and pre-made designs to help us get started quickly.

- In-Store Promotion

    In-store marketing is commonly used in retail stores, and it is another example of below-line activities. For example, visual merchandising, retailing pop-up stores, sampling, point-of-sale (POS) displays, and sales promotions are all effective ways to encourage customers to buy your products and increase your ROIs.

- **Advantages of BTL Marketing**

    Unlike ATL, BTL is very focused on targeting specific ads to certain people, ensuring the content and location line up as clearly as possible with the intent of these potential customers. BTL also differs in that it is much more focused on return on investment (ROI), gaining user conversions, and quantifying success. Instead of simply raising awareness of the brand, BTL is designed to ensure direct consumers for the product or brand, by focusing directly on the user and their wants. This form of engagement marketing is usually easily quantifiable with the advantage of highly trackable results.

III. Through the Line Marketing (TTL)

Finally, we come to through-the-line marketing or TTL marketing. This combines the wider audience and direct approaches of ATL and BTL Marketing, to attempt to both raise brand awareness and target specific potential customers and convert these into measurable and quantifiable sales. One example of this is 360-degree marketing, where you not only have a national TV campaign but supplement this with targeted flyers and newspaper ads.

Another example of TTL Advertising is the use of <u>Digital Marketing</u>, combining online banner ads with social media posts and blogs, for instance.

<u>By implementing these advertising strategies and an integrated marketing approach, you'll be certain to cover a wide of target audiences.</u>

- **Digital Marketing Strategies:**

    <u>Social media platforms are important for through-the-line marketers because they allow them to reach out to customers directly via Facebook, Twitter, Instagram, etc</u>. They also provide interactive media where they can share information about new products and promotions. Through the line, marketers can use these platforms to build relationships with their customers, which helps increase sales in return. More relevantly, digital distribution is important in today's technologically advanced world.

The clear benefit of a TTL approach is that you are attacking two fronts, simultaneously improving general awareness and also aiming to increase traffic and sales.

However, TTL is more expensive to use than either ATL or BTL alone. For this reason, it is normally utilised only by larger and more established companies with the money to back such a large approach.

Module 2

Significance of Marketing Budget, Marketing Calendar and Marketing Plan

Marketing Budget

The marketing budget is a comprehensive financial document that details all income and expenditures for the centre's marketing programme. Marketing budgets are either administered on a cash or accrual basis, or in some likelihood, on both. Income may be budgeted on an accrual basis, in which all the income projected to be received during the year is assumed to be received on an evenly distributed monthly regardless of when it is actually received, and expenses are recorded when they are paid.

- Monthly Marketing Budget and Variance Report

    This report tracks the forecasted and actual income and expenses for the marketing programme on a monthly basis. It provides insights into budget variances, the percentage of total expenses, advertising and promotion expenses as a percentage of retail sales, and net year-to-date performance.

BUDGET	Services
INCOME	Ancillary services, ADVT Boards, Sponsorships, Splay leasing, LED screens etc

BUDGET	Services
EXPENSE	Advertising, Promotions and activations, paid ads., print & media, social media tools, associate sponsorships, miscellaneous.
TOTAL EXPENSE	$$$$$$$$$
Net Yr. to date $ %	

- **Marketing Plan:**

    It's a marketing instrument based on the calendar of marketing programs and activities planned throughout the year. It's a strategy which encompasses all the parameters of marketing, leasing, operational know-how, and competition analysis, all zeroed in on modern analytical skills like SWOT, which gives a realistic opportunity for further improvement on the existing product or platform.

    The clinical start to the marketing plan starts right from the trade area whilst demographics and psychographics are analytical inputs that let the management understand any demographic changes or the opening of any store within the competitive mall, which could cannibalise potential business or the concentration of new residential areas in the vicinity, etc. Then the shoppers intercept within the mall give an opinion of the shoppers, which is very important for any new developments that the centre management is planning to do.

    Once the situation analysis has been fully covered and understandable, qualitative objectives are established upon which new strategies are developed and planned. Ideally, the marketing plan should comprise the following parameters:

1. **Executive Summary:** Provide a concise overview of the marketing plan, highlighting key objectives, strategies, and expected outcomes.

2. **Situation Analysis:** Situation analysis helps to formulate a shopping centre decision-making process by looking at the external and internal factors

impacting its overall success. Performing a situation analysis is essential to every project planning process as it helps identify a centre's **strengths, weaknesses, and growth opportunities** within the trade area against the surrounding competitive Shopping centres.

3. **Market Overview**: Analyse the current market conditions, including trends, competition, and consumer behaviour.

4. **Trade Area Assessment**: Evaluate the demographics and psychographics of the trade area, considering recent changes, new store openings, or residential developments.

5. **Shopper Intercept**: Gather opinions and insights from shoppers within the mall to understand their preferences and expectations for new developments.

6. **Marketing Objectives:** By clearly defining the specific marketing objectives, for example, increasing footfall by 10%, driving sales growth by 15%, and enhancing customer loyalty by 20%.

   Example: Increase footfall by organising engaging events and implementing targeted marketing campaigns that resonate with the target audience.

   a) **Target Audience:** Identify and define the specific target audience, considering demographics, psychographics, and consumer behaviour patterns.

      Example: Target tech-savvy millennials aged 18-30 who are fashion-conscious and value sustainability.

   b) **Brand Positioning:**

      Determine the desired market position for the shopping centre and develop strategies to effectively communicate and reinforce that positioning.

      Example: Position the mall as a trendy and eco-friendly shopping destination that offers a unique mix of sustainable fashion brands.

c) **Marketing Strategies:**

d) **Digital Marketing:**

Developing a comprehensive digital marketing strategy, including website optimisation, SEO, social media campaigns, influencer partnerships, and targeted online advertising.

e) **Traditional Marketing:**

Plan and execute traditional marketing tactics, such as print advertisements, radio spots, billboards, and direct mail campaigns.

7. **Events and Promotions**: Organise engaging events, exclusive previews, and special promotions to attract and retain customers.

Example: Launch a social media campaign showcasing sustainable fashion trends, collaborate with local influencers to promote eco-friendly brands, and organise a fashion show featuring sustainable collections.

a. **Budget Allocation:**

Allocate the marketing budget across different channels and initiatives based on their expected effectiveness and ROI.

Example: Allocate 40% of the budget to digital marketing, 30% to events and promotions, and 30% to traditional marketing.

b. **Marketing Calendar:**

A marketing calendar is more than a simple timeline or schedule — it's a comprehensive strategic tool, a roadmap coordinating all marketing activities for a particular campaign. These calendars are prepared for a full year or a quarter at a minimum, although they must be flexible enough to accommodate any shifts and changes that could occur during the campaign. Marketing calendars serve as the backbone of campaign execution. They provide day-by-day, week-by-week, month-by-month, and even quarter-by-quarter plans that drive the campaign towards its objectives. Realistically, the marketing calendar sets the rhythm for the campaign, outlining key target dates for content creation, publication, and promotional efforts.

Example: Create a sustainable fashion week in September, collaborate with a local charity for Earth Day in April, and launch a back-to-school campaign in August.

c. **Creative Assets:**

Develop visually appealing and engaging creative assets, including visuals, videos, graphics, and compelling copywriting.

Example: Create a series of short videos featuring sustainable fashion tips and showcase eco-friendly products through high-quality visuals.

d. **Measurement and Analytics:**

Establish relevant KPIs to measure the success of marketing initiatives, such as footfall, sales growth, customer engagement, and social media metrics.

Example: Track website traffic, social media engagement, and sales conversion rates to assess the effectiveness of the sustainable fashion campaign.

e. **Monitoring and Reporting:**

Implement a system to monitor the progress of marketing activities and generate regular reports to evaluate performance and make data-driven decisions.

Example: Provide monthly reports highlighting key metrics, campaign performance, and actionable insights for continuous improvement.

f. **Collaboration and Partnerships:**

   Identify potential collaborations and partnerships with complementary businesses or organisations to enhance the shopping centre's visibility and reach.

   Example: Partner with local environmental organisations for joint initiatives, and collaborate with sustainable fashion influencers for co-branded promotions.

g. **Crisis Management:**

   Develop a plan to address potential issues or emergencies that may arise, ensuring clear communication channels and protocols are in place.

   Example: Establish a crisis communication team, outline response procedures, and monitor online sentiment to address any negative publicity promptly.

h. **Evaluation and Review:**

   Conduct periodic evaluations and reviews of the marketing plan to assess its effectiveness and make necessary adjustments.

   Example: Conduct quarterly reviews to analyse campaign performance, gather customer feedback, and stay updated on industry trends, besides the other operational marketing models given below in the table:

1.	Date/Year the Mall Opened
2.	Type of the Centre
3.	GLA
4.	Anchors / Department stores
5.	Key Tenants / Retail Groups
6.	Current year sales per sq. ft
7.	Next year's projection
8.	Occupancy percentage in terms of GLA
9.	Occupancy percentage projected next year
10.	Issues / Concerns
11.	Market share
12.	Tenancy mix percentage of current year
13.	Tenancy mix of next year, any improvements suggested to the existing
14.	Competition within the trade area and secondary market
15.	Any changes in the Demographics compared to last year?
16.	Customer profiling
17.	Disposable Income any variance.
18.	Dual time spent by the shopper within the mall/department store.
19.	Social media analysis reports.
20.	KPIs entrusted to the team.

** The marketing plan also should include supporting documents like;

- Annual budget
- Advertising plan
- Sales promotion plan
- Calendar of events
- Trade Area map
- Demographic information
- Potential retail sales report (GAFO) general apparel furniture and other.
- Income projected

The marketing plan is a comprehensive tool which envisages long-term gain if done with proper strategy and tactical planning while taking into consideration all the coordinates discussed above.

II) Marketing Calendar

There are times when it is essential for a centre to boost its brand recognition or achieve sales projections with the help of marketing activations and sales promotions.

They are an integral part of the well-being of the centre in enhancement of its brand value and, in return, bringing in projected dollars. They are an important part of the annual marketing plan. The events are lined up all along the calendar year in such a way that they cover and celebrate all forms of festivities, talent shows, fashion events, community events and fundraisers, seasonal decor, and sales promotions.

The main purpose is to attract shoppers, drive sales, develop brands, create public awareness, strengthen landlord-tenant relationships, assist leasing efforts in bringing prospective tenants, and finally realise the main objectives of the landlord in increasing income generation and enhancing the brand value of the property.

Marketing events and promotions have come a long way from yesteryears, where from a simple pianist enriching the crowds to dance and folk lore, military bands playing flute and drums enthusiastically to the crowd, field operas it moved to the new era where talent shows where one gets to showcase his or her talent, festive music and shows during festivities took the centre stage, professional commercialisation came into the centre through host of shows like fashion and accessories show, Talk live shows started trending to the digital world where sales promos were held electronically to sizeable coupon driven shoppers, along with community exhibitions and promotions, the landlord and it's centre management gave impetus to broad meaning to marketing activations. *This not only achieved the desired but also made shopping centres a second home to the shoppers within the community.*

Some of the below-listed events are time-tested, have been runaway successful in the past, and still continue to be successful. They are:

Annual Marketing Calendar - Example

January | February | March	Activities, Clearance sale, Markdowns from earlier winter sales. Valentines Day, Mall Décor, Any last-minute additions
April | May | June	New Season Offerings, Virtual Merchandising, Mall Sale Promotion, Spring, Easter Regular Price Event (RPE), Seasons Sale vide Malls Summer Holidays Promotions initiative, Mother's Day, Father's Day.
July | August | September	Clearance of Summer season stock, Back to School promotions, RPE.
October | November | December	Autumn Sale Discount sale 30%, Part Markdowns, Festive Season promotions, Sale Event, Season Decor, Winter Clearance Sales.

- **Marketing Strategy:**

    A shopping centre's sales - Marketing plan, describes the strategies the mall management will deploy to attract and retain tenants and bring in more shoppers to these stores.

    Preparing a plan is critical to success because shopping malls compete with each other and with other retail clusters, such as shopping centres. In cosmopolitan areas, consumers have numerous choices of brands within the stores and the physical and internal shopping centre's ambiance together with other entertainment and dining options. Implementing a sound plan enables a centre to build its competitive edge.

- **Setting Goals:**

    A marketing plan for any business should include goals for the upcoming year. In a marketing plan, a key goal is the sales levels you want your tenants collectively to achieve. Setting up a goal for occupancy percentage annually, together with the amount of available retail space that is occupied by tenants, is the foremost and primary function of the marketing as it ensures a steady forecasted rental income from the operating tenants. When operating to maximum, occupancy allows shoppers to visit the centre and its shopping precincts, which has a direct impact on the growth in sales. With these goals in place, we can track our progress over the course of the year.

- **Determining Target Markets:**

The centre ownership and the management comprising the marketing team must have a clear understanding of the target markets they want to reach and attract to the mall. The demographic characteristics of the area and its factors, such as age and income level, give a fair idea of the potential customer base. Also, a close look at the existing and current customers and whether there are additional groups we want to target.

- **Securing and Retaining Tenants:**

The marketing plan details the strategies and action plans the centre will use to find the right mix of tenants that fits the purchasing behaviour and needs of its target markets. Shoppers coming to the property to visit one store may find other stores appeal to them as well, necessitating some care into finding the right mix.

The centre's management should devise tenant satisfaction strategies, such as conducting an annual survey of tenants to find out what they think the mall is doing really well and areas where the mall could provide better service.

**Helping Increase Business

The more the Shopping Centers marketing team can do to help the stores reach out to customers, the more successful the stores and the mall will be. A marketing strategy must determine the media that will be used to advertise the centre and its stores.

- **Marketing Fund Pool:**

  Many shopping centre's collect marketing funds collectively from the tenants to organise quality events, either for festivals, holidays, or seasonal activities, to attract sizable footprints to the centre. It's not that every store or retailer is well versed in marketing to increase sales. Also, the centre management prefers to host activities as an umbrella for most of the retailers to run a successful marketing campaign there by increasing the sales of the tenants and being accountable for the role the management performs.

  * The marketing calendar is prepared in tandem with the marketing association, with innovative and exponential strategies to help the tenants succeed by planning events and special promotions to build visitor traffic and create publicity opportunities for the centre.

- **Branding & Positioning the Shopping Centre:**

  The marketing and promotional strategies should make the centre stand out.

  Ads could focus on the unique stores we have, the excitement at the centre, the spectacular design and layout of the centre, or the offerings in dining and entertainment that recreate a clear, experiential look and feel and the perfect message for the newspaper and magazine advertising. Besides, boosting social media to connect with the loyal customer base can attract younger shoppers.

  Ultimately, the aim is to create a brand image for the centre, differentiating it from other competitive shopping centres and providing a superior shopping experience.

Marketing KPI'S

The marketing objectives in the form of KPIs are to increase shopping centre sales, which are classified into the following parameters, and the marketing team has to work and analyse accordingly:

Shopping Centre Management - Marketing

1. Sales Promotions

2. Advertising

3. Public Relations and Publicity

4. Centre Positioning

5. Branding

6. Merchandising and distribution

7. Surveys.

8. Digital and Social Media

- **Marketing Objective and Goals:**

    i) To increase the centre's value by increasing the sale of the shopping centre and thereby increasing the sales of the tenants. The growth, for instance, is at 3 percent annually.

    ii) **Advertising and Branding:** The advertising events and sales promotions should have a common theme and objective.

    iii) **Trade Area:**

    To revisit the trade area and analyse and identify any opportunity to increase the shopping centre yield.

    iv) **Demographics:**

    Updated profile of the consumers and shoppers within the trade area and their shopping habits and to identify the gap in shopping centres' penetration.

v) **Shopping Habits and Increase In Dual Time Spending:**

All efforts are to be made to improve and increase the dual time and study the shopping habits of the shoppers, so that the increase in the dual time will be an increase in the spend and growth in sales.

vi) **Surveys and Research:**

The marketing team has to ensure at least two surveys are done in a month to understand the wish list of shoppers in terms of improvement in Tenancy Mix. Also the survey should cover price points, fashion trends which are key attributes for the overall growth.

vii) **Media:**

The marketing team will measure and identify which medium of media is most effective in reaching shoppers within the particular trade area and to measure the result of the targeted activities. The events and the activations will be measured as per the targeted activities and the media support.

viii) **Sponsorship:**

The marketing team is advised that for two major events they have to find a sponsor so that the overall expenditure can be brought down. Besides, finding out the opportunities to enter a partnership deal with business partners annually, which will enhance the shopping centre's growth.

ix) **Speciality leasing:** The marketing team has been given a target to generate substantial revenue by speciality leasing.

Module 3

Digital Marketing

Any marketing that uses electronic devices and can be used by marketing specialists to convey promotional messaging and measure its impact through your customer journey. In practice, digital marketing typically refers to marketing campaigns that appear on a computer, phone, tablet, or other device. It can take many forms, including online video, <u>display ads</u>, search engine marketing, paid social ads, and social media posts. Digital marketing is often compared to "traditional marketing" such as magazine ads, billboards, and <u>direct mail</u>. Oddly, television is usually lumped in with <u>traditional marketing</u>.

Did you know that more than three-quarters of Americans go online on a daily basis? Not only that, but 43% go on more than once a day, and 26% are online "<u>almost constantly</u>."

These figures are even higher among mobile internet users. 89% of Americans go online at least daily, and 31% are online almost constantly. As a marketer, it's important to take advantage of the digital world with an online advertising presence by building a brand, providing a great customer experience that also brings more potential customers, and more with a digital strategy.

A digital marketing strategy allows you to leverage different digital channels—such as social media, pay-per-click, search engine optimization, and email marketing—to connect with existing customers and individuals interested in your products or services. As a result, you can build a brand, provide a great customer experience, bring in potential customers, and more.

Inbound Marketing versus Digital Marketing

Digital marketing and inbound marketing are easily confused, and for good reason. Digital marketing uses many of the same tools as inbound marketing—email and online content, to name a few. Both exist to capture the attention of prospects through the buyer's journey and turn them into customers. But the two approaches take different views of the relationship between the tool and the goal.

Digital marketing considers how individual tools or digital channels can convert prospects. A brand's digital marketing strategy may use multiple platforms or focus all of its efforts on one platform. For example, a company may primarily create content for social media platforms and email marketing campaigns while ignoring other digital marketing avenues.

On the other hand, inbound marketing is a holistic concept. It considers the goal first, then looks at the available tools to determine which will effectively reach target customers, and then at which stage of the sales funnel that should happen. As an example, say you want to boost website traffic to generate more prospects and leads. You can focus on search engine optimisation when developing your content marketing strategy, resulting in more optimised content, including blogs, landing pages, and more.

The most important thing to remember about digital marketing and inbound marketing is that as a marketing professional, you don't have to choose between the two. In fact, they work best together. Inbound marketing provides structure and purpose for effective digital marketing to digital marketing efforts, making sure that each digital marketing channel works towards a goal.

Importance of Digital marketing

Any type of marketing can help your business thrive. However, digital marketing has become increasingly important because of how accessible digital channels are. In fact, there were five billion internet users globally in April 2022 alone.

From social media to text messages, there are many ways to use digital marketing tactics in order to communicate with your target audience. Additionally, digital marketing has minimal upfront costs, making it a cost-effective marketing technique for small businesses.

B2B versus B2C Digital marketing

Digital marketing strategies work for B2B (business-to-business) as well as B2C (business-to-consumer) companies, but best practices differ significantly between the two. Here's a closer look at how digital marketing is used in B2B and B2C marketing strategies.

- B2B clients tend to have longer decision-making processes and, thus, longer sales funnels. Relationship-building strategies work better for these clients, whereas B2C customers tend to respond better to short-term offers and messages.

- B2B transactions are usually based on logic and evidence, which is what skilled B2B digital marketers present. B2C content is more likely to be emotionally-based, focusing on making the customer feel good about a purchase.

- B2B decisions tend to need more than one person's input. The marketing materials that best drive these decisions tend to be shareable and downloadable. B2C customers, on the other hand, favour one-on-one.

Types of Digital Marketing

There are as many specialisations within digital marketing as there are ways of interacting using digital media. Here are a few key examples of the different types of digital marketing tactics.

- Search Engine Optimisation

    Search engine optimization or SEO , is technically a marketing tool rather than a form of marketing in itself. The Balance defines it as **"the art and science of making web pages attractive to search engines."**

The "art and science" part of SEO is what's most important. SEO is a science because it requires you to research and weigh different contributing factors to achieve the highest possible ranking on a search engine results page (SERP).

Today, the most important elements to consider when optimising a web page for search engines include:

- Quality of content

- Level of user engagement

- Mobile-friendliness

- Number and quality of inbound links

In addition to the elements above, you need to optimise technical SEO, which is all the back-end components of your site. This includes URL structure, loading times, and broken links. Improving your technical SEO can help search engines better navigate and crawl your site.

The strategic use of these factors makes search engine optimisation a science, but the unpredictability involved makes it an art.

Ultimately, the goal is to rank on the first page of a search engine's result page. This ensures that those searching for a specific query related to your brand can easily find your products or services. While there are many search engines, digital marketers often focus on Google since it's a global leader in the search engine market.

- **Content Marketing**

  As mentioned, the quality of your content is a key component of an optimised page. As a result, SEO is a major factor in content marketing, a strategy based on the distribution of relevant and valuable content to a target audience.

  As in any marketing strategy, the goal of content marketing is to attract leads that ultimately convert into customers. But it does so differently than traditional advertising. Instead of enticing prospects with potential value from a product or service, it offers value for free in the form of written material, such as:

- Blog posts

- E-books

- Newsletters

- Video or audio transcripts

- Whitepapers

- Infographics

Content marketing matters, and there are plenty of stats to prove it:

- 84% of consumers expect companies to produce entertaining and helpful content experiences

- 62% of companies that have at least 5,000 employees produce content daily

- 92% of marketers believe that their company values content as an important asset

As effective as content marketing is, it can be tricky. Content marketing writers need to be able to rank highly in search engine results while also engaging people who will read the material, share it, and interact further with the brand. When the content is relevant, it can establish strong relationships throughout the pipeline.

Regardless of which content you create, it's a good idea to follow content marketing best practices. This means making content that's grammatically correct, free of errors, easy to understand, relevant, and interesting. Your content should also funnel readers to the next stage in the pipeline, whether that's a free consultation with a sales representative or a sign-up page.

- **Social Media Marketing**

    Social media marketing means driving traffic and brand awareness by engaging people in discussions online. You can use social media marketing to highlight your brand, products, services, culture, and more. With billions of people spending their time engaging on social media platforms, focusing on social media marketing can be worthwhile.

    The most popular digital platforms for social media marketing are Facebook, Twitter, and Instagram, with LinkedIn and YouTube not far behind. Ultimately, which social media platforms you use for your business depends on your goals and audience. For example, if we want to find new leads for any startup, targeting your audience on LinkedIn is a good idea since industry professionals are active on the platform. On the other hand, running social media ads on Instagram may be better for your brand if you run a B2C focused on younger consumers.

    Because social media marketing involves active audience participation, it has become a popular way of getting attention. It's the most popular content medium for B2C digital marketers at 96%, and it's gaining ground in the B2B sphere as well. According to the Content Marketing Institute, 61% of B2B content marketers increased their use of social media this year.

    Social media marketing offers built-in engagement metrics, which are extremely useful in helping you understand how well you're reaching your audience. You get to decide which types of interactions mean the most to you, whether that means the number of shares, comments, or total clicks to your website.

    To create an effective social media marketing strategy, it's crucial to follow best practices. Here are a few of the most important social media marketing best practices:

    - Craft high-quality and engaging content.

    - Reply to comments and questions in a professional manner.

- Create a social media posting schedule.

- Post at the right time.

- Hire social media managers to support your marketing efforts.

- Know your audience and which social media channels they're most active on.

- Pay-per-click marketing.

Pay-per-click or PPC, is a form of digital marketing in which you pay a fee every time someone clicks on your digital ads. So, instead of paying a set amount to constantly run targeted ads on online channels, you only pay for the ads individuals interact with. How and when people see your ad is a bit more complicated.

One of the most common types of PPC is search engine advertising, and because Google is the most popular search engine, many businesses use Google Ads for this purpose. When a spot is available on a search engine results page, also known as a SERP, the engine fills the spot with what is essentially an instant auction. An algorithm prioritises each available ad based on a number of factors, including:

- Ad quality

- Keyword relevance

- Landing page quality

- Bid amount

PPC ads are then placed at the top of search engine result pages based on the factors above whenever a person searches for a specific query.

Each PPC campaign has one or more target actions that viewers are meant to complete after clicking an ad. These actions are known as conversions, and they can be transactional or non-transactional. Making a purchase is a conversion, but so is a newsletter signup or a call made to your home office.

Whatever you choose as your target conversions, you can track them via your chosen digital marketing channels to see how your campaign is doing.

- Affiliate marketing

    Affiliate marketing is a digital marketing tactic that lets someone make money by promoting another person's business. You could be either the promoter or the business who works with the promoter, but the process is the same in either case.

    It works using a revenue sharing model. If you're the affiliate, you get a commission every time someone purchases the item that you promote. If you're the merchant, you pay the affiliate for every sale they help you make.

    Some affiliate marketers choose to review the products of just one company, perhaps on a blog or other third-party site. Others have relationships with multiple merchants.

- Influencer marketing

    Like affiliate marketing, influencer marketing relies on working with an influencer–an individual with a large following, such as a celebrity, industry expert, or content creator–in exchange for exposure. In many cases, these influencers will endorse your products or services to their followers on several social media channels.

    Influencer marketing works well for B2B and B2C companies who want to reach new audiences. However, it's important to partner with reputable influencers since they're essentially representing your brand. The wrong influencer can tarnish the trust consumers have with your business.

Marketing Automation

Marketing automation uses software to power digital marketing campaigns, improving the efficiency and relevance of advertising. As a result, you can focus on creating the strategy behind your digital marketing efforts instead of cumbersome and time-consuming processes.

According to statistics:

- 90% of US consumers find personalisation either "very" or "somewhat" appealing
- 81% of consumers would like the brands they engage with to understand them better
- 77% of companies believe in the value of real-time personalisation, yet 60% with it

Marketing automation lets companies keep up with the expectation of personalisation. It allows brands to:

- **Collect and analyse consumer information**
- **Design targeted marketing campaigns**
- **Send and post digital marketing messages at the right times to the right audiences.**
- **Email Marketing**

  The concept of email marketing is simple—you send a promotional message and hope that your prospect clicks on it. However, the execution is much more complex. First of all, you have to make sure that your emails are wanted. This means having an opt-in list that does the following:

  - Individualises the content, both in the body and in the subject line
  - States clearly what kind of emails the subscriber will get

- An email signature that offers a clear unsubscribe option

- Integrates both transactional and promotional emails

- **Mobile marketing**

  Mobile marketing is a digital marketing strategy that allows us to engage with our target audience on their mobile devices, such as smartphones and tablets. This can be via SMS and MMS messages, social media notifications, mobile app alerts, and more.

- **Benefits Of Digital Marketing :**

  Digital marketing has become prominent largely because it reaches such a wide audience of people. However, it also offers a number of other advantages that can boost marketing efforts, <u>below are a few of the benefits of digital marketing</u>.

  o **A broad geographic reach**

  When you post an ad online, people can see it no matter where they are (provided you haven't limited your ad geographically). This makes it easy to grow your business's market reach and connect with a larger audience across different digital channels.

  o **Cost efficiency**

  Digital marketing not only reaches a broader audience than traditional marketing but also carries a lower cost. Overhead costs for newspaper ads, television spots, and other traditional marketing opportunities can be high. They also give you less control over whether your target audiences will see those messages in the first place.

  With digital marketing, we can create just one content piece that draws visitors to your blog as long as it's active. We can create an email marketing campaign that delivers messages to targeted customer lists on a schedule, and it's easy to change that schedule or the content if need be.

To sum it all up, digital marketing gives much more flexibility and customer response for the ad. spend.

o **Quantifiable Results**

To know whether our marketing strategy works, we need to find out how many customers it attracts and how much revenue it ultimately drives. But how do we do that with a non-digital marketing strategy? There's always the traditional option of asking each customer, "How did you find us?"

Unfortunately, that doesn't work in all industries. Many companies don't get to have one-on-one conversations with their customers, and surveys don't always get complete results. With digital marketing, results monitoring is simple. Digital marketing software and platforms automatically track the number of desired conversions that we get, whether that means email open rates, visits to our home page, or direct purchases.

o **Easier Personalisation**

Digital marketing allows us to gather customer data in a way that offline marketing can't. Data collected digitally tends to be much more precise and specific.

Increase Communication Channel With Customers

Digital marketing lets us communicate with the customers in real-time. More importantly, it lets them communicate with us. Think about the social media strategy. It's great when the target audience sees our latest post, but it's even better when they comment on it or share it. It means more buzz surrounding our product or service, as well as increased visibility every time someone joins the conversation.

- **Digital Marketing Strategy**

   For many small businesses and beginner digital marketers, getting started with digital marketing can be difficult. However, one can create an effective digital marketing strategy to increase brand awareness, engagement, and sales by using the following steps as our starting point.

   o **Set SMART Goals**

   Setting specific, measurable, achievable, relevant, and timely (SMART) goals is crucial for any marketing strategy. While there are many goals we may want to achieve, focus on the ones that will propel our strategy forward instead of causing it to remain stagnant.

   o **Identifying the Audience**

   Before starting any marketing campaign, it's best to identify the target audience; it could be the group of people you want your campaign to reach based on similar attributes, such as age, gender, demographic, or purchasing behaviour. Having a good understanding of your target audience can help you determine which digital marketing channels to use and the information to include in your campaigns.

   o **Create a budget**

   A budget ensures we are spending money effectively towards our goals instead of overspending on digital marketing channels that may not provide the desired results. Consider SMART goals and the digital channel we're planning to use to create a budget.

   o **Select Digital Marketing Channels**

   From content marketing to PPC campaigns and more, there are many digital marketing channels we can use to our advantage. These digital marketing channels often depend on your goals, audience, and budget.

o **Refine Marketing Efforts**

> Make sure to analyse the campaign's data to identify what was done well and areas for improvement once the campaign is over. This allows us to create even better campaigns in the future.

- **Digital Marketing Creates Growth**

Digital marketing should be one of the primary focuses of almost any business's overall marketing strategy. Never before has there been a way to stay in such consistent contact with the customers, and nothing else offers the level of personalisation that digital data can provide. The more we embrace the possibilities of digital marketing, the more we'll be able to realise our company's growth potential.

Key Takeaways

- Digital marketing involves marketing to consumers through digital channels, including websites, mobile devices, and social media platforms.

- This form of marketing is different from internet marketing, which is exclusively done on websites.

- Digital marketing relates to attracting customers via email, content marketing, search platforms, social media, and more.

- One of the biggest challenges digital marketers' faces is how to set themselves apart in a world that is oversaturated with digital marketing ads.

- Digital marketing comes with various challenges, including implicit bias.

Key Performance Indicators (KPIs) in Digital Marketing

KPIs are quantifiable ways that companies can measure long-term performance of marketing and compare their efforts to those of their competition. Areas of measurement include corporate strategies, financial goals and achievements, operational activities, and even marketing campaigns.

The following are some of the most common KPIs that marketers can use to help companies achieve their goals:

- **Blog Articles:** Marketers can use this KPI to figure out how many times a company publishes blog posts each month.

- **Clickthrough Rates:** Companies can use this KPI to figure out how many clicks take place for email distributions. This includes the number of people that open an email and click on a link to complete a sale.

- **Conversion Rate:** This measure focuses on call-to-action promotional programmes. These programs ask consumers to follow through with certain actions, such as buying a product or service before the end of a promotional period. Companies can determine the conversion rate by dividing successful engagements by the total number of requests made.

- **Traffic on social media:** This tracks how many people interact with corporate social media profiles. It includes likes, follows, views, shares, and/or other measurable actions.

- **Website Traffic:** Marketers can use this metric to track how many people visit a company's website. Corporate management can use this information to understand whether the site's design and structure contribute to sales.

Digital Marketing Challenges

Digital marketing poses special challenges for its purveyors. Digital channels proliferate rapidly, and digital marketers have to keep up with how these channels work and how they're used by receivers. Marketers need to know how to use these channels to effectively market their products or services.

It's becoming more difficult to capture receivers' attention because they're increasingly inundated with competing ads. Digital marketers also find it challenging to analyse the vast troves of data they capture and then exploit this information in new marketing efforts.

Module 4

Customer Experience And Engagement

Objective: <u>To increase footfall, enhance the value of the property, and strengthen tenant and management relations by providing exceptional customer experiences and engaging shoppers effectively.</u>

This module would cover the following topics:

- **Understanding Shopper Behaviour:** Analysing shopper demographics, preferences, and behaviour to tailor marketing efforts and offerings.

- **Creating Memorable Experiences:** Developing strategies to create immersive and memorable experiences through events, activations, and interactive elements.

- **Customer Service Excellence:** Implementing customer service training for shopping centre staff to ensure positive interactions with shoppers.

- **Loyalty Programmes:** Designing and implementing loyalty programmes to incentivise repeat visits and increase customer retention.

- **Feedback and Surveys:** Collecting shopper feedback through surveys and feedback mechanisms to identify areas for improvement.

- **Community Engagement:** Establishing community engagement initiatives to build a strong connection with the local community.

- **Tenant Support:** Assisting tenants in improving their offerings and customer engagement to drive their revenue growth.

Understanding Shopper Behaviour

Conducting Market Research:

Shopping centre management should conduct market research to gather essential data about their target audience, including demographics, preferences, shopping habits, and spending behaviour.

This information helps in creating targeted marketing campaigns and improving the overall shopping experience. For example, conducting surveys and focus groups can provide valuable insights into what shoppers are looking for and their expectations from the shopping centre.

1. **Persona Development:** Creating customer personas involves defining typical profiles of shoppers based on their characteristics, interests, and needs. For instance, a shopping centre might identify.

   personas like "Busy Professionals," who value convenience and efficiency, or "Fashion Enthusiasts," who seek trendy and unique stores. Tailoring marketing strategies and offerings based on these personas ensures that the shopping centre can effectively engage with its various customer segments.

2. **Journey Mapping:** Mapping out the shopper's journey involves understanding the various touchpoints and interactions a customer has from the moment they enter the shopping centre until they leave.

   This process helps identify potential pain points and opportunities for improvement. For instance, if shoppers tend to avoid a specific area of the mall, journey mapping can reveal possible reasons such as poor signage or lack of attractive stores.

Creating Memorable Experiences

1. **Event Planning and Execution**: Organising events and activations can attract shoppers and create memorable experiences. For example, hosting seasonal festivals, live performances, or themed events can draw in more footfall and generate excitement and interest.

2. **Immersive Installations**: Implementing interactive installations and art displays can create a unique and attractive atmosphere within the shopping centre. For instance, a digital art installation or a pop-up store with engaging elements can encourage shoppers to explore and spend more time in the mall.

3. **Seasonal and Themed Campaigns**: Developing campaigns around specific seasons or themes, such as back-to-school promotions, holiday celebrations, or cultural festivals, can keep the shopping centre fresh and relevant throughout the year. These campaigns can offer exclusive discounts, incentives, or entertainment to attract shoppers.

Customer Service Excellence

The ability of service providers to consistently meet and exceed customer expectations, optimise key objectives for operational efficiency, enhance experiences through innovative strategies, foster a high-performance, quality team environment, and continually identify and implement process improvements to ensure seamless shopping centre operations and sustained growth—the below key factors help in achieving customer excellence, which is the hallmark for any business or establishment to be successful.

1. **Training Programs**: Providing comprehensive training to shopping centre staff on customer service skills and standards is crucial for creating a positive and welcoming environment. Well-trained staff can assist shoppers effectively, answer queries, and address any issues promptly.

2. **Handling Complaints and Feedback**:

   Properly addressing customer complaints and feedback is essential for maintaining shopper satisfaction.

   When handled professionally and efficiently, complaints can turn into opportunities to enhance customer loyalty.

Loyalty Programs

1. **Loyalty Point Systems:** Implementing loyalty programs that reward shoppers with points for each purchase or visit can encourage repeat visits and higher spending. These points can be redeemed for discounts or special rewards, motivating shoppers to return to the mall.

2. **Exclusive Benefits**: Offering exclusive benefits to loyal customers, such as early access to sales, VIP events, or personalised offers, can make them feel valued and appreciated, further increasing their loyalty to the shopping centre.

Feedback and Surveys

1. **On-Site Surveys**: Placing on-site surveys or digital kiosks throughout the shopping centre can capture real-time feedback from shoppers about their experiences, preferences, and suggestions for improvement.

2. **Online Feedback Mechanisms:** Implementing online feedback mechanisms, like social media polls or email surveys, can reach a broader audience and provide valuable insights into customer satisfaction and preferences.

Community Engagement

1. **Local Partnerships:** Collaborating with local businesses, organisations, and influencers can create cross-promotional opportunities and community events. For instance, partnering with a nearby restaurant for a food festival can attract both their customers and shopping centre visitors.

2. **Social Responsibility Initiatives**: Engaging in social responsibility initiatives, such as supporting local charities or environmentally friendly practices, can strengthen the shopping centre's reputation as a responsible and caring community member.

Tenant Support

1. **Retailer Workshops**: Organising workshops and training sessions for tenants on customer service, visual merchandising, and marketing can help improve their offerings and enhance the overall shopping experience.

2. **Co-marketing Opportunities**: Partnering with tenants on joint marketing campaigns, such as a mall-wide sale or a collective promotion, can drive foot traffic and benefit both the shopping centre and its tenants.

By incorporating these strategies into the shopping centre management's approach, they can effectively increase footfall, enhance property value, and foster strong tenant and management relations while providing exceptional customer experiences and engaging shoppers effectively.

Module 5

Data-Driven Marketing And Performance Analysis

Objective: To increase revenue for tenants and optimise marketing efforts by leveraging data-driven strategies and conducting thorough performance analysis. Data-driven marketing and performance analysis in the context of shopping centre management is crucial for making informed decisions, optimising marketing efforts, and enhancing the overall performance of the shopping centre and its tenants.

1. **Data Collection and Analysis:**

    - **Footfall Analysis:** Shopping centres can use various technologies, such as footfall counters, Wi-Fi tracking, or video analytics, to collect data on the number of visitors and their movement patterns within the mall. This data helps identify peak hours, popular areas, and areas that need improvement.

    - **Shopper Behaviour:** Implementing customer behaviour tracking tools can provide insights into how shoppers interact with the shopping centre, including dwell time, navigation paths, and popular stores. This information helps understand shopper preferences and interests.

    - **Sales Data:** Integrating point-of-sale systems from individual stores in the shopping centre can provide valuable data on sales trends, popular products, and the overall performance of tenants.

2. **Data-Driven Decision Making:**

    - **Marketing Campaigns:** Utilising data insights on shopper behaviour and preferences, shopping centres can tailor marketing campaigns to target specific customer segments effectively. For example, based on shopper demographics, the mall can promote certain events or offers to appeal to their interests.

    - **Tenant Support:**

    Data analysis can help shopping centre management identify areas where tenants might need support, such as improving store layouts or enhancing product offerings, to drive revenue growth.

3. **Performance Metrics and KPIs:**

    - **Footfall Conversion Rate:** This metric measures the percentage of shoppers who make purchases compared to the total footfall. It helps assess the effectiveness of marketing strategies and tenant offerings in converting foot traffic into sales.

    - **Tenant Sales Performance:** Tracking each tenant's sales performance allows shopping centre management to identify top-performing stores and areas for improvement.

    - **Return on Marketing Investment (ROMI):** Evaluating the return on investment from marketing campaigns and promotions helps assess their effectiveness and allocate resources wisely.

4. **A/B Testing and Optimisation:**

    A/B testing (also known as split testing) is the process of comparing two versions of marketing activations or other marketing assets and measuring the difference in performance.

    How is it done? We do this by giving one version to one group and the other version to another group. Then we can see how each variation performs. It's like a competition, pitting two versions of our asset against one another to see which comes out on top.

- **Marketing Campaigns:** Shopping centres can conduct A/B testing for various marketing elements, such as promotional messaging, visuals, or call-to-action buttons, to identify which variations yield the best results in terms of footfall and sales.

- **Tenant Support:** Implementing A/B testing for tenant store layouts or product displays can help optimise their performance and customer engagement.

5. **Marketing Attribution:**

   - **Channel Attribution:** Analysing the impact of different marketing channels (e.g., social media, email, print advertising) on footfall and sales helps allocate marketing budgets effectively.

   - **Event Attribution:** Identifying the impact of specific events or promotions on footfall and tenant revenue helps plan future successful activities.

6. **Business Intelligence Tools:**

   Business intelligence (BI) refers to the procedural and technical infrastructure that collects, stores, and analyses the data produced by a company's activities.

   - **Data Visualisation:** Implementing data visualisation tools like Tableau or Power BI can help shopping centre management create interactive dashboards that provide clear insights from complex datasets.

   - **Predictive Analytics:** Using predictive analytics tools, shopping centres can forecast footfall trends, shopper behaviour, and tenant sales, enabling proactive decision-making.

7. **Performance Review and Reporting:**

   - **Monthly Reports:** Regularly generating comprehensive reports based on data analysis and performance metrics allows shopping centre management to review marketing efforts and tenant performance.

   - **Stakeholder Reports:** Providing data-driven reports to tenants and other stakeholders fosters transparency and collaboration in achieving mutual goals.

8. **Continuous Improvement:**

   - **Data-Driven Feedback:** Encouraging feedback from shoppers and tenants based on data insights can help shopping centres continuously refine their strategies and offerings.

   - **Iterative Approach:** Adopting an iterative approach to marketing and tenant support allows shopping centre management to make gradual improvements based on data analysis and feedback.

<u>These two modules address the shopping centre's objectives of increasing footfall, boosting tenant revenue, enhancing property value, and fostering strong tenant and management relations. By focusing on customer experience and engagement and data-driven marketing, shopping centre management can optimise their efforts to achieve their marketing objectives effectively.</u>

QUESTIONS AND ANSWERS SESSION - MARKETING

Q1: What are the main objectives of shopping centre marketing?

A1: The main objectives of shopping centre marketing include increasing footfall, promoting tenant sales, enhancing brand awareness, attracting new shoppers, and fostering customer loyalty.

Q2: What are some examples of above-the-line (ATL) marketing activities used in shopping centres?

A2: Examples of ATL marketing activities in shopping centres include television advertisements, radio spots, billboards, and newspaper/magazine advertisements.

Q3: How can digital marketing be utilised in shopping centre marketing strategies?

A3: Digital marketing can be used in shopping centre marketing strategies through various channels, such as social media marketing, email marketing, influencer partnerships, search engine optimisation (SEO), and online advertising.

Q4: What are the key components of a marketing plan for a shopping centre?

A4: The key components of a marketing plan for a shopping centre include situation analysis, target audience identification, marketing objectives, brand positioning, marketing strategies (both digital and traditional), budget allocation, marketing calendar, measurement and analysis methods, and crisis management protocols.

Glossary

Marketing

1. **Marketing Strategies:** Comprehensive plans and tactics devised to promote a shopping centre's brand, attract visitors, increase footfall, and enhance tenant engagement and satisfaction.

2. **Digital Marketing:** Marketing efforts conducted through digital channels, such as websites, social media platforms, email campaigns, and online advertisements, to reach and engage the target audience.

3. **Marketing Budget:** The allocated funds and resources designated for marketing activities, promotions, events, and campaigns within a shopping centre.

4. **KPIs (Key Performance Indicators) for Marketing:** Specific metrics used to measure the effectiveness and success of marketing initiatives, such as footfall, sales conversion rates, customer satisfaction, and social media engagement.

These definitions provide a foundational understanding of key terms and concepts used throughout the handbook, enabling professionals in shopping centre management to navigate the content effectively and make informed decisions.

This Handbook is designed to provide a helpful and informative overview of the topics covered. It is not intended to be a substitute for more extensive learning that can be achieved through attending ICSC educational programs and reading additional ICSC professional publications.

You Write. We Publish.

To publish your own book, contact us.

We publish poetry collections, short story collections, novellas and novels.

contact@thewriteorder.com

Instagram- thewriteorder

www.facebook.com/thewriteorder

Shopping Centre Management - Accounting And Finance

M. Nauman Thakur

Contents

Module 1: Scope And Objectives In Accounting And Finance	1
• Executive Summary	1
• Scope	1
• Objectives	1
• Key Considerations	3
• Conclusion	4
• Budget And Types Of Budgets In Shopping Centre Management	4
• Key Considerations In Budget Preparation	5
Module 2: Revenue Streams In Shopping Centres	7
Module 3: Management Information System (Mis) In Accounting	9
• Monthly Report In Shopping Centre Management	9
• Financial Statements	11
Module 4: Variance Report And Components	15
• Accounting Glossary	16
• Questions And Answers Session - Accounting And Finance	17
Appendix	21
• Shopping Centre Management Insurance Checklist	22
Glossary	23
• Finance And Accounting	23

Module 1

Scope And Objectives In Accounting And Finance

Executive Summary

Accounting and finance play a crucial role in the management of shopping malls. They provide essential tools and processes for recording financial transactions, analysing performance and making informed decisions. This document outlines the essentials of accounting and finance in shopping mall management, including its scope, objectives, and key considerations.

Scope

The scope of accounting and finance in shopping mall management encompasses various areas, including revenue recognition, expense accounting, financial statement preparation, budgeting and monitoring, internal control, financial analysis, lease accounting, common area maintenance charges, tenant receivables, service charge accounting, and capital expenditure planning. It involves the systematic recording, analysis, and reporting of financial information to support decision-making and ensure compliance with regulatory requirements.

Objectives

One of the primary objectives of accounting and finance in shopping centre management is to maintain accurate and comprehensive financial records. This includes recording income, expenses, assets, and liabilities in accordance with established accounting principles and standards. By maintaining proper books of accounts, mall management can track financial transactions, monitor cash flow, and ensure transparency in financial reporting.

- **Performance Evaluation:** Accounting and finance facilitate the evaluation of the mall's financial performance. By analysing financial statements and key performance indicators, managers can assess profitability, liquidity, solvency, and efficiency to identify areas for improvement. Performance evaluation helps in benchmarking against industry standards, identifying trends, and making strategic decisions to enhance the mall's financial position.

- **Compliance and Regulatory Reporting:** Another key objective is to ensure compliance with financial regulations and reporting requirements. This involves adhering to accounting standards, tax laws, and other applicable regulations to provide transparent and accurate financial information to stakeholders, including investors, lenders, and regulatory bodies. Compliance with regulations helps to maintain the mall's reputation, build investor confidence, and avoid legal repercussions.

- **Budgeting and Planning**: Accounting and finance assist in the preparation and monitoring of budgets. By forecasting revenue and expenses, setting financial targets, and monitoring actual performance against budgeted figures, mall management can make informed decisions and control costs effectively. Budgeting and planning help in resource allocation, identifying financial gaps, and aligning financial strategies with the mall's objectives.

- **Risk Management:** Accounting and finance contribute to the identification, assessment, and management of financial risks in shopping mall operations. This includes establishing internal controls, implementing risk mitigation strategies, and maintaining appropriate insurance coverage to safeguard assets and minimise potential losses. Risk management ensures the mall's financial stability, protects against fraud and theft, and enhances operational efficiency.

- **Decision Support**: Accounting and finance provide relevant and reliable information for decision-making. Through financial analysis, managers can evaluate investment opportunities, assess the financial viability of expansion projects, negotiate leases, and determine pricing strategies. By providing accurate and timely financial information, accounting and finance enable informed decision-making, reducing uncertainty and maximising returns.

Key Considerations

In the context of shopping mall management, several key considerations must be taken into account:

a) **Lease Accounting:** Shopping malls typically lease spaces to tenants. Proper lease accounting is crucial to ensure accurate recognition of rental income and expenses, adherence to lease terms, and compliance with lease accounting standards. Lease accounting involves recording lease agreements, determining lease classifications, and recognising lease-related revenues and expenses by accounting standards such as IFRS 16.

b) **Common Area Maintenance (CAM) Charges:** Mall management may need to allocate and track CAM charges to tenants based on their proportional usage of common areas. Accurate accounting and reporting of CAM charges ensure fair allocation and transparency in financial dealings. It involves calculating CAM charges, issuing invoices, tracking collections, and reconciling CAM expenses.

c) **Tenant Receivables and Collections:** Monitoring and managing tenant receivables is crucial to maintaining healthy cash flow. Accounting systems should enable tracking tenant invoices, monitoring payment schedules, and managing collections effectively. Clear policies and procedures for handling outstanding tenant balances, collection efforts, and dispute resolution should be in place.

d) **Service Charge Accounting:** Shopping malls often charge tenants for additional services such as maintenance, security, and utilities. Proper service charge accounting ensures accurate recording and allocation of service charges to tenants. This involves tracking service charge expenses, reconciling costs, and issuing invoices based on agreed-upon service charge rates.

e) **Capital Expenditure Planning**: Mall management requires careful planning and budgeting for capital expenditures, such as renovations, equipment upgrades, and infrastructure improvements. Accounting and finance play a crucial role in evaluating the financial feasibility of capital projects, assessing return on investment, and allocating funds efficiently.

Conclusion

Accounting and finance are essential components of shopping mall management. They provide the necessary tools and processes for financial record-keeping, performance evaluation, compliance, budgeting, risk management, and decision support. By adhering to accounting standards, implementing robust financial controls, and leveraging financial information, mall management can optimise financial performance, mitigate risks, and enhance stakeholder confidence. Effective accounting and finance practices contribute to the overall success and sustainability of shopping malls in a dynamic and competitive marketplace.

Budget and Types of Budgets In Shopping Centre Management

A budget refers to a financial plan that outlines the projected income and expenses associated with operating and maintaining the mall. It is a crucial tool for effective financial management and helps ensure that resources are allocated appropriately to meet the operational and strategic goals of the shopping mall.

There are typically two types of budgets in shopping mall management:

- **Operating Budget:** This budget focuses on day-to-day expenses and income related to the mall's operations. It includes items such as staffing costs, utilities, maintenance, marketing expenses, security, and other operational expenses. The operating budget helps mall management track expenses and ensure that the mall's daily operations run smoothly.

- **Capital Budget:** The capital budget is concerned with long-term investments and major expenditures that improve or expand the shopping mall's infrastructure and facilities. It includes funds allocated for renovations, construction, equipment upgrades, and other capital projects. The capital budget helps the management plan for future growth and enhance the overall shopping experience for customers.

Key Considerations in Budget Preparation

- **Revenue Projections:** Analysing historical data, market trends, and tenant agreements to forecast rental income and other revenue streams accurately.

- **Expense Estimates:** Evaluating past expenses, current cost structures, inflation rates, and market conditions to estimate operating expenses, such as maintenance, utilities, staffing, and marketing costs.

- **Capital Expenditure** Planning: Identifying capital improvement projects, renovations, and equipment purchases and estimating their costs and impact on the budget.

- **Contingency Planning:** Allowing for unexpected expenses, contingencies, or economic fluctuations by including a reserve or contingency fund in the budget.

- **Operation Budget**: The operation budget includes day-to-day operating expenses, such as salaries, utilities, maintenance, security, and administrative costs.

- **Marketing Budget:** The marketing budget focuses on promotional activities, advertising, events, and campaigns to attract customers, increase footfall, and enhance the shopping centre's brand image.

- **Reports Prepared by the Accounts Department:** The accounts department prepares various reports, including:

    i) **Income Statements:** Summarises the shopping centre's revenues, expenses, and profitability over a specific period.

ii) **Balance Sheets:** Presents the shopping centre's assets, liabilities, and equity at a specific point in time, providing a snapshot of its financial position.

iii) **Cash Flow Statements:** Shows the inflows and outflows of cash, providing insights into the shopping centre's liquidity and ability to meet its financial obligations.

Module 2

Revenue Streams In Shopping Centres

- **Rental Income:** The primary revenue stream for shopping centres is rental income from leasing retail spaces to tenants. The shopping centre earns revenue through base rent, which is a fixed amount paid by tenants for occupying the space.

- **Percentage Rent:** In addition to base rent, shopping centres often have a percentage rent clause in lease agreements. This means that tenants pay a percentage of their sales revenue as rent, usually after a certain threshold is met. It allows the shopping centre to benefit from the success of its tenants.

- **Common Area Maintenance Charges (CAM):** Shopping centres may charge tenants CAM fees to cover the costs of maintaining and operating common areas such as parking lots, walkways, restrooms, and common seating areas. These charges help generate additional revenue for the shopping centre.

- **Ancillary Income:** Shopping centres can generate income from various ancillary sources, including fees for services provided to tenants, such as advertising and marketing services, event organisation, or facility management. Other sources of ancillary income can include vending machines, ATMs, or kiosks within the shopping centre.

- **Parking Fees:** Many shopping centres charge parking fees to visitors. Depending on the location and demand, these fees can contribute significantly to the revenue stream.

- **Advertising and Sponsorship:** Shopping centres can partner with brands or businesses for advertising and sponsorship opportunities within the mall. This can include digital signage, banners, promotional events, or naming rights for specific areas within the shopping centre.

- **Food Courts and Restaurants:** Shopping centres often have food courts or restaurants within their premises. Revenue is generated through rental income as percentage rentals if the sales exceed the agreed terms and conditions, from these food and beverage establishments.

- **Specialty Leasing**: Shopping centres may offer short-term leasing opportunities to businesses for kiosks, carts, or pop-up shops. These temporary lease agreements provide additional revenue and bring diversity to the tenant mix.

- **Increase in the Leasable Area through RE-Development of the Existing Area:** In some cases, shopping centres may undertake property development projects within their premises, such as adding new retail spaces, entertainment venues, or office spaces. Upon completion, these additional developments can be leased at a premium rental.

KEY TAKEAWAYS: It's important to note that the revenue streams can vary depending on factors such as the location, size, and type of shopping centre, as well as prevailing market conditions. Shopping centre management actively seeks to maximise revenue from these sources while maintaining a balanced tenant mix and delivering a positive shopping experience for visitors.

Module 3

Management Information System (MIS) In Accounting

MIS refers to a system that collects, processes, stores, and disseminates information to support decision-making and management activities within an organisation. In the context of accounting, MIS focuses on the use of technology and information systems to gather, analyse, and present financial data to assist in managerial decision-making.

MIS in accounting helps provide timely and accurate financial information to management, enabling them to monitor and control various aspects of the organisation's financial performance. It typically involves the use of software applications and databases to gather and process data, generate reports, and support financial analysis.

The MIS in accounting can include functionalities such as financial reporting, budgeting and forecasting, cost analysis, inventory management, and performance measurement. It aids in streamlining financial processes, improving data accuracy, and enhancing the overall efficiency of accounting operations.

Monthly Report in Shopping Centre Management

A monthly report in shopping mall management is a document prepared every month to provide an overview of the mall's performance, financial status, and key metrics. It serves as a management tool to assess the progress and make informed decisions regarding the operation of the shopping centre. The content of a monthly report may vary depending on the specific requirements and priorities of management, but it generally includes the following components:

a) **Financial Statements:** The monthly report includes financial statements such as the income statement, balance sheet, and cash flow statement. These statements provide an overview of the mall's financial performance, assets, liabilities, and cash flows during the specific month.

b) **Revenue Analysis:** This section focuses on analysing the sources of revenue generated by the shopping mall during the month. It includes details on rental income from tenants, parking fees, and any other income streams. The analysis may compare the revenue figures to the previous month or the same period in the previous year to identify trends or deviations.

c) **Expense Analysis:** The monthly report includes a breakdown of the various expenses incurred by the shopping mall, such as utilities, maintenance, marketing, staff salaries, and other operational costs. The analysis helps track and monitor expenditure patterns, identify areas of cost savings, and manage the budget effectively.

d) **Occupancy and Tenant Analysis:** This section provides an overview of the occupancy status of the shopping mall, including the percentage of leased spaces, vacancy rates, and tenant turnover. It may also include details on new lease agreements, tenant renewals, or any significant changes in the tenant mix.

e) **Key Performance Indicators (KPIs):** The monthly report may incorporate key performance indicators relevant to shopping mall management. These KPIs would include footfall (number of visitors), sales per square foot, tenant sales performance, customer satisfaction ratings, or any other metrics deemed important by the management.

f) **Operational Highlights:** The report may highlight significant operational achievements, challenges, or events that occurred during the month. It can include updates on marketing campaigns, tenant promotions, facility maintenance activities, or other operational initiatives.

The monthly report on shopping mall management aims to provide a comprehensive snapshot of the mall's financial performance, operational status, and key metrics. It enables management to evaluate the effectiveness of strategies, identify areas for improvement, and make data-driven decisions to enhance the overall performance of the shopping mall.

Financial Statements

The three key financial statements are:

- **Income Statement (also known as the Profit and Loss Statement or Statement of Comprehensive Income):** An income statement provides a summary of a company's revenues, expenses, gains, and losses over a specific period, typically on a quarterly or annual basis. It shows the company's financial performance by detailing its ability to generate profit or incur losses during that period. The income statement starts with the company's revenues, which include sales of goods or services, interest income, and other income sources. Then, it subtracts various expenses, such as the cost of goods sold, operating expenses (e.g., salaries, rent, utilities), depreciation, interest expenses, and taxes. The result is the net income or net loss for the period, which indicates the company's profitability.

- **Balance Sheet (also known as the Statement of Financial Position):** A balance sheet provides a snapshot of a company's financial position at a specific point in time, usually at the end of a reporting period, such as a fiscal quarter or year. It presents a company's assets, liabilities, and shareholders' equity, showcasing its financial health and indicating its overall net worth. The balance sheet follows the fundamental accounting equation:

    Assets = Liabilities + Shareholders' Equity.

    Assets represent what the company owns, such as cash, accounts receivable, inventory, property, and equipment. Liabilities represent what the company owes to others, such as loans, accounts payable, and accrued expenses. Shareholders' equity represents the residual interest in the company's assets after deducting its liabilities. It includes common stock, retained earnings, and additional paid-in capital.

- **Cash Flow Statement:** A cash flow statement shows the inflow and outflow of cash and cash equivalents during a specific period, typically broken down into operating activities, investing activities, and financing activities. It provides insights into a company's ability to generate cash and its liquidity position. The cash flow statement begins with the net cash flow from operating activities, which includes cash received from sales, interest, dividends, and cash paid for expenses, suppliers, salaries, taxes, and other operating costs. It then shows the net cash flow from investing activities, which includes cash used for acquiring or selling assets, investments, or subsidiaries.

Finally, it presents the net cash flow from financing activities, which includes cash from issuing or repurchasing stocks, issuing or repaying debt, and paying dividends. The cash flow statement helps assess a company's ability to generate cash from its core operations, invest in growth or capital expenditures, finance its operations, or repay debts. It is a valuable tool for understanding a company's cash flow dynamics and its ability to meet financial obligations.

Shopping Mall Name XYZ
Income Statement
For the Period Ending [Date]
Rental Income:
Base Rent
Percentage Rent
Other Rental Income
Total Rental Income
Other Revenue:
Parking Fees
Advertising and Sponsorship Income
Ancillary Income (e.g., vending machines, kiosks)
Event Income
Other Miscellaneous Income

Total Other Revenue
Operating Expenses:
Utilities
Maintenance and Repairs
Security
Marketing and Advertising
Staff Salaries and Benefits
Administrative Expenses
Property Management Fees
Other Operating Expenses
Total Operating Expenses
Net Operating Income
Depreciation Expense
Interest Expense
GST / Tax
Other Expenses
Net Income (loss)
Balance Sheet
As of [Date]
Assets:
Current Assets
- Cash and Cash Equivalents
- Accounts Receivable (from tenants)
- Prepaid Expenses
- Other Current Assets
Property, Plant, and Equipment
- Land
- Buildings
- Leasehold Improvements
- Furniture and Fixtures
- Equipment
- Accumulated Depreciation
Intangible Assets

- Leasehold Rights
- Goodwill
- Other Intangible Assets
Other Assets
- Investments
- Deferred Charges
- Other Miscellaneous Assets
Total Assets
Liabilities:
Current Liabilities
- Accounts Payable (to vendors)
- Accrued Expenses
- Current Portion of Long-term Debt
- Other Current Liabilities
Long-term Liabilities
- Long-term Debt
- Deferred Tax Liabilities
- Other Long-term Liabilities
Total Liabilities
Shareholders' Equity:
Common Stock
Retained Earnings
Additional Paid-in Capital
Total Shareholders' Equity
Total Liabilities and Shareholders' Equity

Module 4

Variance Report And Components

A variance report in shopping centre finance is a document that compares actual financial results to budgeted or expected figures. It identifies and analyses the differences or variances between the two, highlighting areas where the actual performance deviates from the planned or desired outcomes. The purpose of a variance report is to provide insights into the reasons behind the variances and to facilitate decision-making and corrective actions.

Key components of a variance report in shopping centre finance may include:

- **Budgeted Amount:** This column represents the original budgeted or expected amount for a specific financial metric, such as revenue, expenses, or profit.

- **Actual Amount:** This column shows the actual financial result achieved during the reporting period.

- **Variance:** The variance column calculates the difference between the actual amount and the budgeted amount. It indicates whether the result is higher (positive variance) or lower (negative variance) than expected.

- **Percentage Variance:** This column expresses the variance as a percentage, enabling a quick assessment of the magnitude of the variance relative to the budgeted amount.

- **Analysis and Commentary:** The report typically includes a section for analysing and explaining the variances. It may provide insights into the factors contributing to the variances, such as changes in market conditions, unexpected expenses, or deviations in performance from the original plan.

- **Action Plan:** In some cases, a variance report may include a section for proposing corrective actions to address the variances. This helps management identify opportunities for improvement, cost-saving measures, or adjustments to strategies to align with the financial goals.

"Variance reports are useful tools for monitoring and managing the financial performance of a shopping centre. They provide a clear picture of how the actual results compare to the budgeted expectations, helping stakeholders understand the reasons behind any deviations and enabling informed decision-making to optimise financial outcomes."

ACCOUNTING GLOSSARY

An income statement, also known as a profit and loss statement or statement of earnings, provides a summary of a company's revenues, expenses, and net profit or loss over a specific period. Here are the key components typically included in an income statement:

Revenue: This section displays the total sales or revenue generated by the company during the specified period. It includes revenue from the sale of goods or services, as well as any other operating income.

Gross Profit: Gross profit is calculated by subtracting the COGS from the revenue. It reflects profitability before considering operating expenses.

Operating Expenses: This section includes all expenses incurred in the ordinary course of business operations. It typically includes categories such as:

- **Marketing Expenses:** Costs related to sales promotions, advertising, marketing campaigns, and salaries or commissions for sales staff.

- **General and Administrative Expenses:** Costs associated with the overall management and administration of the company, including salaries of non-sales employees, office rent, utilities, and legal fees.

- **Research and Development (R&D) Expenses:** Costs incurred in developing new products, improving existing products, or conducting research activities.

- **Depreciation and Amortisation:** Expenses allocated to account for the gradual reduction in value of long-term assets or the amortisation of intangible assets.

- **Operating Income or Operating Profit:** Operating income is derived by subtracting the total operating expenses from the gross profit. It represents the profit earned from the core operations of the business.

  - **Non-Operating Income and Expenses:** This section includes any income or expenses that are not directly related to the core business operations. It may include interest income, interest expenses, gains or losses from investments, and other non-operating items.

  - **Net Income or Net Profit:** Net income is calculated by subtracting non-operating expenses from the operating income. It represents the final profit earned by the company after accounting for all expenses and income. The income statement provides valuable insights into a company's financial performance, including its ability to generate revenue, manage costs, and generate profits. It is an essential component of financial reporting and analysis, aiding in decision-making, benchmarking, and evaluating the overall profitability of the business.

QUESTIONS AND ANSWERS SESSION - ACCOUNTING AND FINANCE

Q1: What is the primary objective of accounting and finance in shopping mall management?

1A: The primary objective is to maintain accurate and comprehensive financial records.

2Q: How do accounting and finance contribute to performance evaluation in shopping malls?

2A: Accounting and finance help assess profitability, liquidity, solvency, and efficiency to identify areas for improvement.

3Q: Why is compliance with financial regulations and reporting requirements important in shopping mall management?

3A: Compliance ensures transparency, maintains the mall's reputation, builds investor confidence, and avoids legal repercussions.

4Q: What role do accounts and finance play in budgeting and planning for shopping malls?

4A: They assist in forecasting revenue and expenses, setting financial targets, and monitoring actual performance against the budget.

5Q: How do accounting and finance contribute to risk management in shopping mall operations?

5A: They establish internal controls, implement risk mitigation strategies, and maintain appropriate insurance coverage to safeguard assets

6Q: How do accounting and finance support decision-making in shopping mall management?

6A: They provide relevant and reliable financial information for evaluating investment opportunities, expansion projects, leases, and pricing strategies.

7Q: What is lease accounting, and why is it important in shopping mall management?

7A: Lease accounting involves recording lease agreements, determining lease classifications, and accurately recognising rental income and expenses.

8Q: Why is accurate accounting and reporting of Common Area Maintenance (CAM) charges essential for shopping malls?

8A: Accurate accounting and reporting ensure fair allocation and transparency in financial dealings regarding proportional usage of common areas.

9Q: How do accounting and finance contribute to managing tenant receivables in shopping malls?

9A: They enable tracking tenant invoices, monitoring payment schedules, and implementing effective collection strategies to maintain healthy cash flow.

10Q: What role does account and finance play in capital expenditure planning for shopping malls?

10A: They evaluate the financial feasibility of capital projects, assess return on investment, and allocate funds efficiently for renovations and improvements.

Appendix

G1	This monthly analysis of accounts receivable helps determine if the collection effort is being performed prudently. This report provides an overall review of collection activities.

Accounts Receivable Aging Report

Tenant	Total	Current	30-60 Days	61-90 Days	91+ Days	Comments
	$0.00					
	$0.00					
	$0.00					
	$0.00					
	$0.00					
	$0.00					
	$0.00					
	$0.00					
	$0.00					
	$0.00					
	$0.00					
	$0.00					
	$0.00					
	$0.00					
	$0.00					
	$0.00					
	$0.00					
	$0.00					
	$0.00					
	$0.00					
	$0.00					
	$0.00					
	$0.00					
	$0.00					
Total	$0.00	$0.00	$0.00	$0.00	$0.00	

Shopping Centre Management - Accounting And Finance

Shopping Centre Management Insurance Checklist

Accounts and Finance

E3 — This form provides a list of those areas that should be considered when studying your insurance needs.

Insurance Program Checklist

- ☐ **Property Insurance**
  - ☐ **Risks To Be Insured**
    - ☐ Buildings
    - ☐ Business Interruption/Rental Income
    - ☐ Personal Property: Furniture, Fixtures, Equipment, Income
    - ☐ Data Processing Equipment
    - ☐ Property in Transit
    - ☐ Property of Others for Which You Are Responsible
    - ☐ Materials to be Used in Construction
    - ☐ Boiler and Machinery
    - ☐ Plate Glass
  - ☐ **Coverage Aspects**
    - ☐ All Risk or Named Perils
    - ☐ Earthquake
    - ☐ Flood
    - ☐ Demolition; Increased Cost of Construction; Contingent Liability from Changes in Building Laws
    - ☐ Replacement Cost or Actual Cash Value
    - ☐ Coinsurance or Stipulated (Agreed) Amount
    - ☐ Deductibles
    - ☐ Course of Construction: Theft
    - ☐ Course of Construction: Resultant Damage from Faulty Workmanship and Error in Design
    - ☐ Rental Income: Actual Loss Sustained
    - ☐ Boiler, Machinery, Mechanical Breakdown

- **Liability Insurance**
  - ☐ **Comprehensive General Liability**
    - ☐ Limits/aggregates (each location)
    - ☐ Personal Injury Exclusions A & C
    - ☐ Broad Form Property Damage
    - ☐ Products and Completed Operations
    - ☐ Owners/Contractors Protective Liability
    - ☐ Blanket Contractual Liability
    - ☐ Owned/Non-Owned/Hired Automobile

Page 1 of 2   E3

-22-

Glossary

Finance and Accounting

1. **Budgets:** Financial plans that outline the expected revenues and expenses of the shopping centre over a specific period, helping in financial management and decision-making.

2. **Revenue Streams:** Various sources of income for the shopping centre, including rental income, percentage rent, common area maintenance charges, advertising, and other ancillary income.

These definitions provide a foundational understanding of key terms and concepts used throughout the handbook, enabling professionals in shopping centre management to navigate the content effectively and make informed decisions.

This Handbook is designed to provide a helpful and informative overview of the topics covered. It is not intended to be a substitute for more extensive learning that can be achieved through attending ICSC educational programs and reading additional ICSC professional publications.

You Write. We Publish.

To publish your own book, contact us.

We publish poetry collections, short story collections, novellas and novels.

contact@thewriteorder.com

Instagram- thewriteorder

www.facebook.com/thewriteorder

Shopping Centre Management - FM Operations

M. Nauman Thakur

Contents

Module 1: Shopping Centre Maintenance   1
- Administration And Management Fees   9

Module 2: Housekeeping Operations   11
- Floor Care   12
- Advantages of Floor Care   12
- The Sweeper And Its Advantages   14
- Executive Housekeeper Role And Responsibilities   14
- Responsibilities   15
- Embrace Green Cleaning   17

Module 3: Security Operations   23
- Inventories And Spillage Management   25
- Standard Operational Procedure For Security Personnel   25
- Role Of Security Manager In A Shopping Centre   34
- Compliance And Regulatory Requirements   35
- Questions And Answers Session - FM Operations   38

Part 2 - FM Operations   43

Module 4: Details About Important MEP Systems   43
- Key Components   43
- Assembly of Chillers And Chiller Yard   45
- Safety And Security   47
- Mechanical Equipment In A Shopping Centre   50
- Electrical Equipment In A Shopping Centre: 50

Module 5: BMS (Building Management System) In A Shopping Centre   53
- Assembly   53
- Fire Suppression Equipment In A Shopping Centre   54

- FM 2000 And Where It Is Used In Shopping Centres   55
- Load Distribution of the HV Transfer In A Shopping Centre   57

Appendix   59

Glossary   69
- FM Operations   69

These modules and subheadings cover a comprehensive range of topics related to FM Operations, housekeeping, and security operations in a shopping centre.

Module 1

Shopping Centre Maintenance

Shopping centre maintenance, or facility management, is the preservation and enhancement of the property through the upkeep of the physical and mechanical systems.

Facility Management can be split into two categories;

1. Hard FM Services

2. Soft FM Services

The former concerns services such as maintenance and plumbing, whereas the latter focuses on services such as cleaning and catering. The easiest way to understand the difference between Hard FM and Soft FM services is to think about facilities management from a people (usage of facilities) and facilities (structure and physical aspects) perspective:

- If the service relates to managing the usage of a facility, **it is Soft FM**.

- If the service relates to managing the physical aspect of a facility, **it is Hard FM**.

Categorising FM services into these two components makes it easier to keep on top of tasks, especially when managing large facility or multiple buildings.

Shopping Centre Management - FM Operations

Hard and Soft FM operations are two categories of facilities management that are typically performed in a shopping centre.

Hard FM operations generally refer to activities that are related to the physical structure and mechanical systems of the building, such as HVAC maintenance, electrical and plumbing repairs, fire safety inspections, and building security. These operations are typically handled by a specialised team of professionals who are trained to address technical issues related to the building's infrastructure.

Soft FM operations, on the other hand, refer to activities that are focused on the comfort and convenience of the building's occupants, such as cleaning, landscaping, pest control, waste management, and general maintenance. These operations are typically performed by a separate team of workers who are responsible for ensuring that the shopping centre is clean, safe, and visually appealing to visitors.

In a shopping centre, both hard and soft FM operations are essential to ensure the smooth functioning of the building and the satisfaction of its tenants and visitors. By managing both the physical infrastructure and the occupant experience, facilities managers can create a welcoming, functional, and safe environment for everyone who uses the space.

A) The systems that fall under **Hard FM** ownership and are accountable for their upkeep are:

• Heating, Ventilation, and air conditioning (HVAC)
• Electrical systems and energy management systems
• Lighting systems
• PA address systems
• Firefighting systems
• Plumbing, Doors and Locks
• Vertical conveying systems like travelators, escalators and lifts
• Roof maintenance
• Parking lots, asphalt areas, interlock curbs and parapets

B) Besides, the systems which falls under **Soft FM** are:

• Security
• Trash removal
• Sweeping parking lots
• Food court operations
• Main Mall signage
• Cleaning of restrooms, atrium common areas and lift lobbies

All the above responsibilities are a process and are programmed or scheduled daily, weekly or annually, besides daily, weekly, or annually. Besides the daily inspection of the facility team, weekly and monthly inspections by the landlord help to achieve and maintain international standards par excellence against competitors.

Property inspection is a detailed inspection of the physical assets of the shopping mall, which helps to understand the health and longevity of the physical parameters of these assets and plan rectification works if required.

All these things are computed and tabled at the start of the financial year in the form of the annual maintenance budget, which allows the shopping mall management to be proactive and plan above-work schedules and annual maintenance services well in time and orderly.

C) **General Maintenance and Inspections**

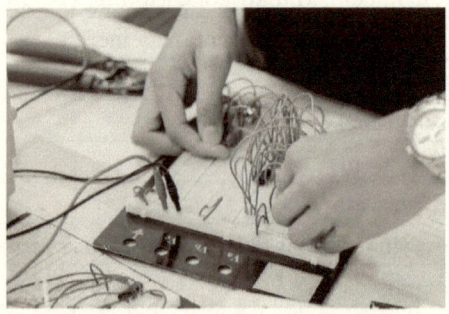

Shopping Centre Management - FM Operations

The mall operations team is normally headed by the Manager and depending upon the ownership whether the maintenance team should be in house or outsource the FM operations as an Annual Maintenance Contract (AMC) normally regional and super regional malls outsource such works due to the enormity of the size of the operations as they have the expertise and skilled labour, technicians in a particular segment of the FM installations and its operations.

Typically such maintenance is of two types

i) Preventive maintenance

ii) Reactive maintenance

1. The Preventive maintenance is an **Annual** maintenance contract and is further classified on daily, weekly, monthly, quarterly, by annually and annually basis as per the requirements of the ownership.

2. Reactive maintenance is to call the vendor on job when something within the equipment breaks down, normally in this case the MOU is signed for such types of maintenance services with the original vendor who has supplied the equipment.

For illustration purpose some of the details are:

1) Daily:

DAILY	HARD / SOFT FM OPERATIONS CHECKLIST
The FM team starts the daily operations from the most frequented areas within & outer - peripheral areas of the Mall.	• The FM team then inspects restrooms, and makes sure that the plumbing fixtures are running properly.

DAILY	HARD / SOFT FM OPERATIONS CHECKLIST
	• Inspection of the ambient temperature within the mall normally 18 -22 degrees is kept by default to maintain cooling and an environment which is refreshing within the mall.
	• Check the flow of the water.
	• All wooden carpentry wooden doors and handles, hinges, food court tables, baby high sitting chairs etc are inspected and repaired, if required.
	• Look out for broken irrigation fixtures to prevent water leaks.
	• Check for any overhead hazards which could cause serious damage to the goodwill of the property, overhead tile, skirting, hangings, skylight glasses etc.
	• Check the parking lots for potholes, broken curbs, damaged humps besides check the parking lights to see none are out and no safety hazards exist.
	• If the Mall is where snow falls, then clear the pathways, entrance ways, parking lots to thwart any potential hazards.

II) Weekly / Monthly - Checklist

Weekly / Monthly	• HVAC systems, electrical and mechanical systems for any possible rectification or replacement of damaged parts
	• Roof waterproofing membrane
	• Check all the fire extinguishers and smoke alarms and panels

	• Check Conveying systems for any possible damage
	• Drain points
	• Water fountains
	• Exterior landscaping

D) Common Area Maintenance

Most maintenance for the common area falls under CAMAC, and is charged to the tenants, depending upon the lease agreements between the tenant and the landlord.

Some examples where CAM is charged for maintaining HVAC, lighting, and parking lots, common areas, walkways, conveying systems, and landscaping, besides not limited to food court operations and waste management, also include management fees and administration fees in most of the leases.

E) ANNUAL PREVENTIVE MAINTENANCE SCHEDULE

F) Annual Maintenance Budget of Shopping Centres

ANNUAL MAINTENANCE FM BUDGET

Housekeeping Cost	Classification	Remarks
1. Cleaning Services for the Mall	Soft	
2. Pest Control	Soft	
3. Housekeeping Skip / Garbage removal (x trip @ */- per trip)	Soft	
4. Housekeeping consumables	Soft	
5. Food Serving Trays	Soft	
II) Engineering		
6. AMCs	Hard	
6.1. MEP	Hard	
6.2. Water Feature	Soft	
6.3. Sewerage removal (2 trips per month @25/- per trip)	Hard	

Housekeeping Cost	Classification	Remarks
6.4. Kitchen hood	Hard	
6.5. CCTV System	Soft	
6.6. Fire Alarm System	Hard	
6.7. BMS System / Lighting control system	Hard	
6.8. Access Control System	Hard	
6.9. Footfall Counting System	Hard	
6.10. Vertical Transportation	Hard	
6.11. Auto Doors	-Hard	
6.12. Landscaping	Soft	
6.13. Fire Fighting System	Hard	
6.14. LPG System	Hard	
6.15. Odour Elimination System	Soft	
6.16. Water Tank cleaning / Lab Test	Soft	
6.17. Drainage Line Cleaning	Soft	
6.18. Aluminium Window Maintenance		
III) Facilities Consumables / Repair & Maintenance		
7. Design & Consultancy (Toilet & Food court)	Soft	
7.2. Repair & Maintenance - General	Soft	
7.3. Repair & Maintenance - Civil	Soft	
7.4. Repair & Maintenance - Electrical	Hard	
7.5. Repair & Maintenance - HVAC	Hard	
7.6. Repair & Maintenance - Plumbing	Hard/ Soft	
7.7. Outdoor signage approval	Soft	
7.8. Profile sheet hoarding		
7.9. Low Current System Spares/ repair - Fire Alarm	Hard	

Shopping Centre Management - FM Operations

Housekeeping Cost	Classification	Remarks
7.10. Low Current System Spares/ repair - SMATV	Hard	
7.11. Low Current System Spares/ repair - BMS	Hard	
7.12. Low Current System Spares/ repair - CCTV	Hard	
7.13. Low Current System Spares/ repair - Access Control	Hard	
7.14. Low Current System Spares/ repair - Footfall	Hard	
7.15. Fire Fighting System Spares/ repair	Hard	
7.16. Vertical Transport Spares (comps, yellow inserts)	Hard/ Soft	
7.17. Scissor Lift / Spider Lift Spares (controller, battery, switch, etc)	Hard/soft	
IV) Utility Charges	Finance	
8. Electricity	Accounts	
8.1. CHW Capacity	Accounts	
8.3. CHW Energy	Accounts	
8.4. Water	Accounts	
8.5. Sewage	Accounts	
8.6. LPG	Accounts	
Digital Tower & Parking Internet OPTIONAL		
LED Screen Installation Govt Approvals ... OPTIONAL		
9. Setup Cost - Mall	Hard / soft / Tenancy Coordination	
Operations Grand Total	$$$$	

G) **Capital Expense:**

Having explained CAM above, we will identify what the capital expenses are, as some of the executives are confused between the two. Any structural improvements, replacement of major equipment, and adding additional features to enhance the property and bring value in either short- or long-term gains are all capital expenses and are the responsibilities of the landlord. However, in some instances, on the insistence of the landlord to get or lease a big box tenant or space created additionally to adjust the requirements of the anchor tenant, there could be special provisions within the lease agreement that, after completion of depreciation, the structure of the big box would be the mall property or as per the understanding documented.

Administration and Management fees

Most of the leases where I have headed the shopping centres there used to be provisions for covering the management and administration fees from the CAM charges.

TPGL (Third party general liability): it's an overall insurance that the Landlord covers at a sum to protect its assets and liabilities and mostly part of the payment is recovered from the tenants for occupying the space.

Module 2

Housekeeping Operations

Housekeeping in a mall is a critical aspect of facility management. The primary goal of housekeeping is to maintain the cleanliness, hygiene, and overall appearance of the shopping centre, ensuring high standards of service and a pleasing experience.

One of the most defining areas that sets various shopping centres apart is the quality of the housekeeping services at the centre. The housekeeping management should have a check list, a daily schedule, and procedures to follow. It's of utmost importance to inspect the exterior and interior common areas daily before the mall opens for business.

The management must have a diligent routine of walking and inspecting the exterior grounds, truck docks, parking areas, back hallways, restrooms, tenant storefronts, common corridors, conveying systems railings, lifts, glass doors, trash cans and fountains. This will assure the manager that the centre is ready for the shoppers and that the environment is free from any hazards.

The management should impart routine workshops and training to the housekeeping personnel on the ethical knowledge and personation of hygiene and enhance their housekeeping skills.

Further, the management should adhere to the checklist and monitor the housekeeping schedules, which should include deployment, change of shifts, routine daily and nightly housekeeping tasks generally include deep cleaning like scrubbing and mopping the atrium of the mall, corridors, restrooms, walkways, pressure washing all the parking lots, scrubbing of oil spillage, cleaning cleaning if the areas where the trays are washed so that there is no grease on the floor which could be a security and accident hazard along the parking lots, cleaning of food court tables and chairs.

Floor Care

The daily tasks normally consist of mopping the corridors, atrium, and lift lobbies intermittently, besides emptying trash or garbage bins on a regular basis, especially in the food court, helping tenants with trays at the food court, clearing the tables, and mopping all food and drink spills immediately.

The above tasks are performed by experienced housekeeping personnel with expertise in using modern housekeeping equipment, such as:

A) Sweepers

B) Vacuum Cleaners

C) Scrubber Dryers

The mall's operating hours and the shoppers' constant presence, therefore floor care, require fast and effective methods for cleaning the common floors, food court, parking lots, lobby entrances, rest rooms and other areas frequented upon to avoid annoying customers with the slow sweeping of brooms and wet rags cleaning of supermarkets and shopping malls is quick and effortless. Halls that are constantly trodden on, food courts where drinks and food fall to the ground, toilets, shelves full of goods, vehicles for restocking warehouses: **the floors of a shopping mall get dirty quickly and must always be cleaned and sanitised.** These large environments, however, make manual cleaning impossible. This is why it is essential to rely on professional products dedicated to floor care.

Advantages OF Floor Care

Cleaning in shopping centres using **vacuum cleaners, sweepers and floor scrubber dryers** allows, first of all, carrying out **cleaning** operations **in the**

presence of customers, as these tools can be used without having to fence the areas to the public.

Nowadays, in the mass retail trade, shops are open to the public twenty four hours a day, so cleaning shifts cannot fence aisles and display areas. With vacuum cleaners, sweepers and scrubber dryers, which are **easy to use**, it is possible to operate even in the presence of customers and shop assistants, intervening immediately and leaving everything clean and dry.

The thousands of footprints walking inside the shopping centre, carry **dust and stones** from outside under their soles every day adds to the **waste produced in the dining areas and toilets**. *The main advantage of the scrubber dryer is to obtain, with a simple passage, a* **deep cleaning**, *offering customers a* **high standard of hygiene**. *At the same time,* **the operation time and annoyance** *caused by cleaning with traditional tools such as brooms, dustpans, mops, trolleys and mops are* **strongly reduced**.

Scrubber dryers are the best tool for **professionally washing and sanitising floors** of all kinds, materials and sizes. By cleaning and drying quickly and thoroughly, these machines ensure floors which are immediately dry and safe, thus preventing areas to be cleaned from being closed for long periods of time or someone from slipping on water residues.

These machines are characterised by the cleaning and abrasive action of **rotating brushes** which dispense a **detergent solution** on the floor to dissolve the dirt. The residual liquid is then collected by a **squeegee** and immediately conveyed into a special tank by a turbine, leaving the floor dry.

Scrubber dryers are divided according to how they are driven:

- **Push (walk-behind) series** are driven by the operator with a handle on the back; they are suitable for the smallest spaces such as small warehouses, offices, conference rooms, refreshment rooms, cafés and all areas up to 500 square metres. Their compactness allows frequent use in limited areas even in the presence of people, where a larger machine would be intrusive.

Easy to use even by unskilled personnel, the scrubber dryers offer enormous advantages over traditional cleaning:

- **They reduce working time** by more than 50%.

- They wash and sanitise floors **without fencing the area to the public**

- **They consume less water and detergent**, achieving a **higher level of hygiene** than conventional washing

- **They leave no marks or stains** on the ground, ensuring an excellent aesthetic result.

The Sweeper And Its Advantages

To **collect coarse dirt and dust from every floor**, the sweeper is the most suitable machine. Thanks to its **side brushes conveying the dirt towards a central roller brush,** the sweeper loads the dirt into a special container, thus eliminating the effort required for manual sweeping, reducing working time, and dispersing dust residues from the broom and dustpan.

Sweepers are also divided into:

- <u>Push (walk-behind) series</u>, compact and agile, suitable for small environments and in the presence of obstacles;

- <u>Ride-on series</u>, powerful and fast, capable of high performance on very large surfaces.

Executive Housekeeper Role And Responsibilities

- Training housekeepers on cleaning and maintenance tasks

- Overseeing staff performance on a daily basis

- Checking rooms and common areas, including stairways and lounge areas, for cleanliness; besides organising employee shifts, training and motivating team members and checking private and public areas for tidiness.

Responsibilities

- Train housekeepers on cleaning and maintenance tasks

- Oversee staff on a daily basis

- Check rooms and common areas, including stairways and lounge areas, for cleanliness

- Schedule shifts and arrange for replacements in cases of absence

- Establish and educate staff on cleanliness, tidiness and hygiene standards

- Motivate team members and resolve any issues that occur on the job

- Respond to customer complaints and special requests

- Monitor and replenish cleaning products stock including floor cleaner, bleach and rubber gloves

- Participate in large cleaning projects as required

- Ensure compliance with safety and sanitation policies in all housekeeping areas.

1. **Cleaning Protocols:**

    Protocols That Housekeeping In Shopping Centres Needs To Follow:

    I. Prevent slips and falls by regularly cleaning and drying floors, using signage for wet areas, and promptly addressing hazards.

    II. Promote fire safety by properly storing flammable materials, keeping fire exits clear, and maintaining fire extinguishers and detectors.

    III. Train staff in safe chemical handling, provide appropriate personal protective equipment (PPE), and ensure proper storage and disposal of cleaning chemicals.

IV. Implement an effective waste management system with separate bins for recyclables, general waste, and hazardous materials.

V. Train staff in proper lifting techniques, provide ergonomic equipment, and encourage breaks and task rotation.

VI. Regularly inspect electrical cords and appliances, ensure proper grounding, and avoid overloading circuits.

VII. Promote good personal hygiene among staff with regular handwashing, the use of sanitizers, and appropriate protective gear.

VIII. Regularly inspect and maintain housekeeping equipment, provide training on its usage, and ensure safe storage.

IX. Implement effective pest control measures to prevent infestations and maintain a hygienic environment.

X. Provide comprehensive safety training programmes, encourage open communication channels, and promptly address safety concerns or incidents.

2. **Cleaning Impact On Shopping Centres:**

The clean shopping centres encourage visitors to shop comfortably and freely, enhancing the overall shopping process and experience. With clean toilets, floor surfaces, glass doors, elevator buttons, handrails, and other frequently touched areas and surfaces, visitors will not be able to obtain diseases and health issues.

They might even spend a lot of time and money on these shopping centres. A lasting good impression can also allow customers to subtly promote the clean shopping centres to their family and friends, which can be a good thing for the owners of shopping centres and retail establishments.

As for the owners of the clean shopping centres themselves, they can surely sustain the operations of their business given that customers support their establishments through frequent visits and spending on goods, increasing and patronising brand identity, and most importantly, loyalty to the particular shopping centre they visit.

Embrace Green Cleaning

In recent years, the retail and hospitality sectors have confronted ecological impacts. The world is already jeopardised by many environmental issues, like global climate change, ozone depletion, pollution, exploitation of resources, and increasing amounts of solid waste. Shopping centres, in some way or another, have been raising their standards of eco-friendliness and are embracing green cleaning to champion and align themselves as sustainable and environmental partners.

Having said that, green cleaning or green housekeeping is an important aspect of sustainable practices, an evolving trend of today's times. This is a comparatively new concept, and the term is used for employing cleaning methods and products that are environment-friendly, i.e., which have ingredients and processes that inherently safeguard human health and environmental quality. Having a 'green cleaning policy' has now become a standard of sorts in the industry. A 'green cleaning policy' involves several aspects, the most important of which is the revaluation of current cleaning products and methods.

LEED (Leadership in Energy and Environmental Design), the world's forerunner in the environmental certification of buildings, has in fact made such a policy a mandatory part of its indoor environmental quality section for certification and recertification. Certain housekeeping practices, like using certified equipment, microfiber cleaning, entryway matting, and water-saving devices, also contribute to the green cleaning movement.

Here are a few steps that the retail and hospitality industries can take to make their housekeeping eco-friendly:

1. Keeping the Chemicals Out

    Shopping centres, hotels, and mixed-use developments are sectors where there is far greater usage of chemicals than in offices or households. While purchasing cleaning products, the housekeeping department must select cleaning products that are least harmful. This will ensure shoppers, consumers, and cleaning staff are safe from exposure to these chemicals. The water run-off from these commercial developments can pollute water sources if toxic cleaning solutions are used. Even fertilisers and pesticides used within these premises must be used safely and minimally. Aerosols and fresheners can be another source of various toxins, such as formaldehyde, benzene, styrene, and phthalates. Therefore, keeping an eye out for natural and safe options is essential.

2. **Use Chemicals Safely**

The chemicals used for cleaning must be handled with vigilance and care. Exposure to harmful chemicals can have a negative impact, mostly on the housekeeping staff, and therefore must be reduced as much as possible. Staff must be provided with adequate equipment such as safety goggles and gloves when working with strong chemicals. Cleaning products must be appropriately diluted. Accidents that cause leakage of chemicals can be quite dangerous; therefore, every chemical must be stored in a secure place.

3. **Clean Green**

A high standard of cleanliness has to be maintained by the establishments; this means continuously making sure surfaces are clean. This pressure demands that effective cleaning options be chosen for the job.

4. **Invest in Green Equipment**

It is high time that the retail and hospitality industries go a step further and invest in green cleaning equipment to use the resources minimally. Sustainable products must be used for floor and carpet care. For example, Green Seal, which provides environmental certification in the US, recommends <u>vacuum cleaners that comply with Carpet and Rug Institute's Green Label Programme requirements and work at a sound level of less than 70 decibels.</u>

5. **Pest Management Plan**

   Pesticides and pest management methods used in the development must be sensitive to the environment. They must have a good indoor integrated pest management (IPM) plan that defines how pests should be managed in such a manner that they are least harmful to humans and the environment. The pesticides picked must be least toxic, preferably natural, and used minimally.

6. **Training Courses for the Staff**

   Having eco-friendly processes and products in place will not make a difference if staff aren't utilising them correctly. This is impacted by each staff member's personal beliefs in regard to environmentally friendly practices, which is why the concerned industry needs to offer training courses for their staff. This initiative will surely help and further aid in conserving water, which might otherwise be wasted due to unnecessary flushing of toilets or excessive use of certain cleaning processes. The great thing about the training course is that it will carry over into other aspects of the staff's lives as well. There are several areas that the retail and hospitality sectors can focus on when it comes to training their staff, including rationalisation, water management, energy efficiency, and water recycling, and as they say, every little step counts.

7. **Technology and Innovations Revolutionising the Housekeeping Industry**

   Technology and innovations have significantly transformed housekeeping operations in centres, making them more efficient, streamlined, and convenient. Some examples include:

   i. **Mobile Applications:** Mobile apps have revolutionised housekeeping operations in shopping centres. Cleaning staff can use mobile apps to receive task assignments, report completed tasks, track inventory, and communicate with supervisors. These apps streamline communication, improve task management, and enhance productivity.

ii. **Robotic Cleaners:** Robotic vacuum cleaners and floor scrubbers have become increasingly popular in shopping centres. These autonomous machines can navigate through aisles, corridors, and open spaces, efficiently cleaning floors and removing debris. They can operate during non-business hours, minimising disruption to shoppers and staff.

iii. **Smart Waste Management:** Smart waste management systems utilise sensors and data analytics to optimise waste collection. Trash bins equipped with sensors can detect the level of waste and send real-time notifications to staff when they need emptying. This data-driven approach improves operational efficiency and reduces unnecessary waste collections.

iv. **Internet of Things (IoT) Integration:** IoT technology allows various devices and systems to connect and share data, enabling centralised control and monitoring. In the context of housekeeping, IoT integration can include smart thermostats for energy optimisation, remote monitoring of HVAC systems, and real-time tracking of cleaning equipment and supplies.

v. **Digital Checklists and Inspections:** Traditional paper-based checklists and inspections have been replaced by digital solutions. Housekeeping staff can use tablets or mobile devices to access electronic checklists and perform inspections. Digital systems can automatically generate reports, flag issues, and track maintenance requests, ensuring timely resolution of cleaning and maintenance tasks.

vi. **Automated Dispensing Systems:** Automated dispensing systems for cleaning supplies and chemicals provide accurate measurements, reduce wastage, and ensure consistent use. These systems can be integrated with inventory management, automatically reordering supplies when needed, and minimising stock outs or excess inventory.

vii. **UV-C Disinfection:** Ultraviolet-C (UV-C) disinfection technology has gained traction in the wake of the COVID-19 pandemic. UV-C light can effectively kill viruses and bacteria, providing an additional layer of disinfection in high-touch areas. Shopping centres can utilise UV-C devices to sanitise surfaces and enhance cleanliness.

viii. **Energy-Efficient Cleaning Equipment:** Innovations in cleaning equipment have focused on energy efficiency, reducing water consumption, and using eco-friendly cleaning agents. Energy-efficient vacuum cleaners, low-flow scrubbers, and green cleaning solutions contribute to sustainability efforts while maintaining cleanliness standards.

ix. **Data Analytics and Predictive Maintenance:** By leveraging data analytics, shopping centres can gain insights into cleaning patterns, foot traffic, and occupancy rates. This information helps optimise cleaning schedules, allocate resources efficiently, and predict maintenance needs, resulting in cost savings and improved customer experience.

x. **Augmented Reality (AR) for Training:** AR technology can assist in training housekeeping staff by overlaying digital information onto the physical environment. Staff can use AR-enabled devices to access training materials, interactive guides, and step-by-step instructions, improving efficiency and accuracy in performing cleaning tasks.

These technological advancements have revolutionised housekeeping operations in shopping centres, enhancing cleanliness, productivity, and customer satisfaction.

Module 3

Security Operations

In an environment like the one we live in today, we ensure our and our loved ones well-being to be safe and keep our homes and properties secure. The same can be said about any establishment or businesses in which we are remotely or actively engaged or associated. Here we are talking about the 'shopping centre industry' which has surged ahead and probably happens to be the second fastest growing economy in India, and as per financial analysts, it could become a trillion-dollar industry by the end of 2032.

Therefore, the security of the property or development has also evolved with the change, and its requirements are continually scaling up by endorsing very high and professional standards, which now include security professionals who can respond to the seemingly incessant demands and unexpected challenges.

The present dynamism of the global economy, which comes with pressures from the demanding analogy of work culture and business ethos it places in the retail workplace, demands that a vigilant security team be in place.

Today's retail security teams are upscaling their skill sets as per the on-going demand, both physically and through technology-based comprehensive training to manage enhanced security protocols to ensure that unexpected incidents are prevented and that a pleasant and safe shopping experience prevails within the shopping centres for the shoppers.

There is great value for property owners who invest in securing their premises. Customers, employees, and visitors are comforted by seeing security personnel, along with integrated video monitoring and other security enhancements.

Keeping shoppers safe and secure during volatile economic and political times requires a partnership between security providers, property owners and managers, and local law enforcement.

I. **Security Engagement**

   The Shopping Centre Security team goes through a cycle of routines and drills to master the art of safety protocols, familiarise themselves with the sensitive and difficult locations, and prepare for any contingency within the mall. The security drill normally conducted in a shopping mall is based on the safety of the owner's property and tenants within the retail precincts. To deal with any untoward crisis, the security personnel of the mall and also of the retail shops (which have their own access control) must be well versed and highly skilled in monitoring and controlling the following:

II. **Access control** of all the entrances leading to the mall and retail shops is by far the most important part of the security drill. As they say, if access control is strong and attentive, then half the battle in the prevention of crime or accidents is resolved.

   1. **Patrolling:** The key to successful and safe mall operations is to be omnipresent within the mall precincts, such as around conveying systems, food courts, mall entrances, curb areas, car parking areas, staircases, basements, storage areas of the mall, etc., to name a few locations. The security patrolling distribution is based on the requirements of the security manager in dealing with crowd management.

   2. **Car Parking Management** has found that more than 50% of incidents occur annually in car parking, especially during peak hours of the mall, caused by security personnel's not being attentive or lax during operational hours, faulty CCTV coverage, faded curb parking or traffic markings, beaten traffic humps, etc.

      <u>The security personnel should be trained in managing the traffic, should have perfect endurance to walk the car parking area, be attentive to the peak hours when there is strong vehicular movement, should record</u>

<u>damage markings or any other traffic-related issues and should be brought forward to the management for immediate rectification.</u>

3. **Thefts Within The Retail Stores**: It's a nuisance that the retailers have to comprehend; however, it can be brought down considerably, by streamlining checklists through training advocacy imparted to the security personnel deployed on account of.

Inventories and Spillage Management

- **Inventories and spillage,** which normally happen in large boxes like hypermarkets and retail anchors besides mom-and-pop stores, if the security personnel are not attentive despite the stores being equipped with CCTV and sensomatics, can still happen through fit-out rooms within the retail store. The security has to be omnipresent and should have agility and flair in understanding shoppers' behaviour or sudden actions.

- In addition to, Fire Drills, Water spillage or any other contingency the security should be well versed with the protocols and procedures.

- To be more efficient and effective in managing security management, the mall management or tenants have to understand the characteristics of risk management more professionally and take every step to fully prove their obligations.

Standard Operational Procedure for Security Personnel

They have been written keeping in mind the nature of duty and protocol and are obligated to follow instructions or command for effective surveillance and security cover to the property and the shoppers visiting the shopping centre:

1. Following Instructions

    - All security personnel and officers are to obey all instructions and commands given by their superior officers either in writing or verbally without fail.

Shopping Centre Management - FM Operations

2. Discipline

   - All security personnel must be disciplined and courteous to all occupants, visitors, the public, superiors and subordinates at all times.

3. Attire of the Security Personnel

   - All security personnel must be in full uniform including headgear whilst on duty. Hair must be kept short and tidy at all times.

4. Work Procedures

   - Security personnel must be attentive at all times.

   - Security personnel are not allowed to be at ease during their time of duty in the Malls | Commercial bldg. or any of the retail shops they are assigned.

   - During duty Security personnel are not allowed to lean against a wall or appear inattentive while they're on duty.

   - The security personnel are not allowed to leave their beat without informing their supervisor or the beat in charge.

   - The security guards are not allowed to sleep while remaining on duty.

   - All incidents met during patrolling by the security personnel are to be logged in the log book and informed to their superior officer or supervisor.

   - Security personnel are not allowed to be under the influence of alcohol or any drugs or found in abbreviated conditions, consume alcohol or be while on duty.

   - All security personnel are not allowed to take into possession or safely keep any properties, stocks, displays, or unattended items whether valuables or not without proper authorisation or means of sales and transfers.

   - Security personnel deputed within the sensitive areas within the mall or control room are not allowed to record proceedings or shoppers within the mall, pass any sensitive information, or record on their cell phones or instruments while on duty unless authorised by the management.

- There will be zero tolerance for any security personnel involved in abuse, entering into a quarrel, fight, or use of abusive language against its management, superiors, shoppers, or colleagues at all times unless their own lives are threatened.

5. **Security and Intelligence check**

It is very important that all the security personnel within the precinct be properly vetted to ensure that they are free from criminal records at the time of their appointment.

6. **Physical and Mental Health**

The security personnel must be physically checked by the physician and a certificate issued from the hospital/physician on their mental and physical fitness so that they can perform their duties diligently.

7. **Security Paraphernalia**

The security apparatus allotted to security personnel deployed for Access Control within shopping malls and commercial areas, should contain a note radio set, identification tag, whistle, LED baton, torchlight, pocketbook, pen raincoats, and, in some cases, umbrellas.

8. **Log Books**

All security personnel must ensure all diaries and record books are kept in good order and produced for verification by their superiors and/or management from time to time.

9. **Incident Record Keeping:**

- It's paramount that the security team record all incidents within the shopping malls wherever they are deployed and are privy to incidents.

The incident report should be comprehensive in detail, including the occurrence, action taken, and follow-up on the directions given by the seniors in attending the incident.

- The incident book should be kept in a proper place and should be numbered properly for reference, together with supporting documentation which could be used in the filing of the incidents with the local authorities subject to the written consent of the management. Also, the incident book should be kept under the custody of the security manager. The supervisor as per the discretion of the order from the mall management.

- All incident reports are to contain the following basic information:

    i. Full name, designation and the identification number of the person submitting the report.

    ii. The date, time and location of the incident.

    iii. Contractors working within the mall or retail shops doing renovation, repair, and maintenance work are required to apply online for out passes through the contractors they fall under. They should have the counter signature of the RDD (retail delivery and development manager) and security manager and should show the pass to the access control in-charge when visiting the mall as per the details and directions mentioned therein, some of which are basic and are found in most of the fit-out passes issued by the security head.

10. **Contractors/Visitors/Log Book** should contain the date, time in and out, full name, identification number, vehicle registration number, purpose of work, and civil identification number. Further, visitors entering after the mall's operational hours are to register with the security guard at the identified entrance during such hours by the mall management security department per the directions issued as per the rules and regulations of the security manual.

11. Besides the above, there are other input registers that the Security, Housekeeping, and Concierge team maintains for mixed-use developments or commercial places.

The following security registers should be maintained:

I. Visitors register:

- Office Open/Close Register

- Security Duty Register

- Security Duty Handover Register

- Attendance Register Housekeeping and Security Staff

- Housekeeping In-Out Register

- Concierge Parcels /Letter Receiving Register

- Gate Entry Register

- Firefighting Mock Drills Register

II. Security SOPs Mixed Use Developments/Commercial Offices and Residential developments security regulations:

- Staff/Casual labourers – Security to identify the person, make an entry in the register and issue the coloured identification badges and will keep a record of the issued badges.

- Housekeeping movements to the respective floors shall be monitored through identification tags.

- Incoming Visitors- Security will confirm with the person whom the visitor wants to meet. If the person is available,

- Security will make an entry in the register and direct him/her to the concerned officials. Visitors who have an appointment with the concerned official shall be greeted by the reception staff and directed to the Security staff only.

- Visitors will be given a visitor badge.

- Visitors are not allowed to enter any workstation as per the company's policies.

- Visitors are requested not to leave their personal baggage at reception.

III. **Material Movements within the Mall | Mixed Use Development:**

- Material coming into the premises must be accompanied by a proper gate pass.

- No item will be taken out without written permission of the department head.

- Documents for material incoming and outgoing should be implemented with a list of authorised signatories.

Shifting of materials from one wing to another should be carefully monitored and a record of such has to be maintained to avoid confusion.

IV. **Mail and Courier Movements:**

- Incoming and outgoing mail/courier records to be maintained properly.

- Incoming – security person will receive the mail and courier and hand it over to the concerned person.

- Outgoing – He will make an entry of outgoing mail/courier with full details for any loss/ missing report and should be given to Admin without delay.

- No courier should be sent out without the seal and sign of the departmental head.

V. **General Patrolling Procedure:**

- The security must ensure that once the shopping centre is closed, all the unwanted lights and Air conditioning units are put off.

- Security should keep a watch on the activities of the casual labourers/contractors. If security finds anything unusual/untoward, a report must be given to the Admin Head/Security Supervisor first verbally (in case urgent) and then in writing.

- Frisking/Checking all outsourced staff shall be thoroughly frisked at the time of their leaving the premises after finishing the work. In case of any resistance from the employee or person, the same will be detained and informed to the concerned authority.

- Garbage being ferried out of the premises by the housekeeping, contractors, and labour personnel must be thoroughly checked before it is taken out. If anything untoward is found it must be reported to the Security Head.

- FM | Housekeeping or any other outsourced personnel should be frisked/checked on their in and out movements.

- Frisking is applicable for all, Vendors, merchandisers, and staff working within or outsourced.

VI. **Handing and Taking Over Shifts by Security Personnel:**

- The guards coming on a concerned shift for duty or going off duty will go through the log and entries of the previous shift and discuss the progress plan with the relieving team or personnel as the case be.

- The security team deployed along with the Security Supervisor should check the entire building thoroughly before the Mall trading hours and after the closing of the Operations of the Mall.

- Security should check all the systems which are in the facility/ under security.

- Occurrences report register to be maintained.

- Shift security team replacing the earlier team should check all the documents, and systems, which are related to security before taking over charge.

VII. Fire Control:

- All the fire equipment is to be checked whether serviceable or unserviceable.

- Security along with the FM team, should know where the fire extinguishers are located/installed and be able to operate them immediately in case of any fire accidents.

- The Security and the vendor should check the expiry of the fire extinguishers and replace them if expired, through the security manager.

- Security should know the location of the Assembly points In case of fire to safeguard the life and property of the Mall or development.

- Employees should take part and be made aware to respond during emergency procedures through mock drills, also route exit plans should be placed as per the fire dept. authorities.

- The Mall management should mention contact details of the Police | Ambulance and Fire services in SOPs and a copy should be provided to the tenants for their use during emergencies.

VIII. Emergency Procedures:

- Security should have all the addresses and contact numbers of the nearest police station, hospital, ambulance, and fire brigade.

- Security will, in case of an emergency, ring the alarm bell or siren and immediately report the situation.

- Security personnel should be well versed in the entire emergency exit door and main entry gate so that they can take suitable action at short notice.

- Security personnel should patrol the car parking area and should be vigilant against illegal car parkers, as it has been reported by the surveillance team that some of the cars get parked for days or months until the owners of such cars return from holidays, or, as the case may be, the security personnel should coordinate with the local police authorities and act as per the protocols mandated by the authorities.

- The security is also responsible for providing a safe route to the moviegoers, especially during the last movie shows of the night.

IX. **Disposal of Lost and Found items:**

- The other important thing that security undertakes, besides other responsibilities, is the disposal of lost and found items left behind by shoppers, which primarily consist of purses, key chains, rings, earrings from the restroom, money, shades or goggles, ID cards, etc., which accumulate over a period of time and require dispensation on the left-over time period as per the Security Manual and in coordination with the local authorities.

X. **Security Paraphernalia:**

The security team should always have the below security equipment and gadgets to look more professional and efficient during their routine operations. Paraphernalia to be more efficient and professional. The procuring department within the mall should always give due diligence to the requisitions from the security manager for including security items and paraphernalia in an annual budget so that there is enough stock of the safety items, like:

1. Q managers for crowd control and in event management roles.

2. LED batons.

3. Cones, barriers, and water barriers

4. Convex car parking mirror for tight corners within the multi-parking

5. Speed limit stickers and traffic humps

6. Mobile audio systems and radio sets

7. Uniforms, belts, and shoes.

Role Of Security Manager in a Shopping Centre

The role of a security manager in a shopping centre is crucial in ensuring the safety and security of the property, its occupants, and visitors. The security manager is responsible for overseeing all security operations within the shopping centre and implementing measures to prevent and respond to potential threats or incidents. Here are some key responsibilities of a security manager in a shopping centre:

Security Planning and Strategy: The security manager develops and implements security plans, strategies, and policies to protect the shopping centre. This includes conducting risk assessments, identifying vulnerabilities, and devising security protocols and procedures.

- **Team Management:** The security manager supervises and manages the security team, including hiring, training, scheduling, and performance evaluation of security personnel. They ensure that the team is adequately staffed, trained, and equipped to handle security challenges.

- **Access Control:** The security manager establishes and maintains access control measures throughout the shopping centre. This involves managing entrance points, monitoring visitor and staff access, implementing ID verification systems, and controlling the flow of people within the premises.

- **Surveillance and Monitoring**: The security manager oversees the installation and operation of surveillance systems, such as CCTV cameras, to monitor activities within the shopping centre. They ensure that security personnel are trained in using surveillance equipment effectively and that monitoring is conducted proactively.

- **Emergency Preparedness:** The security manager develops emergency response plans and coordinates with relevant stakeholders, such as local law enforcement and emergency services. They conduct drills and training sessions to prepare the security team and other staff for various emergency scenarios, such as fire, medical emergencies, or evacuation procedures.

- **Incident Management:** In the event of security incidents or breaches, the security manager leads the response and investigation. They coordinate with security personnel, local authorities, and management to mitigate risks, collect evidence, and implement corrective measures to prevent future incidents.

- **Stakeholder Collaboration**: The security manager collaborates with property owners, tenants, facility managers, and local law enforcement to ensure a safe and secure environment within the shopping centre. They establish partnerships, share information, and coordinate security efforts to address shared concerns and maintain a cohesive security approach.

Compliance and Regulatory Requirements

The security manager ensures compliance with relevant security regulations, laws, and industry standards. They stay updated on security trends, technological advancements, and legal requirements to implement best practices and adapt security measures accordingly.

- **Customer Service**: The security manager fosters a customer-centric approach to security, ensuring that shoppers and visitors have a positive and safe experience within the shopping centre. They handle customer inquiries, complaints, and concerns related to security and work to maintain a welcoming and secure environment.

- **Training and Education**: The security manager provides ongoing training and education to security personnel on topics such as emergency response, conflict resolution, customer service, and security procedures. They promote a culture of continuous learning and professional development within the security team.

Overall, the security manager plays a crucial role in maintaining the security and safety of a shopping centre. They combine strategic planning, operational management, and stakeholder collaboration to ensure effective security measures are in place and to respond efficiently to any security-related incidents or emergencies.

- **Daily Duties Of The Security Manager:**

    The daily chores of a security manager in a shopping centre can vary depending on the specific needs and circumstances of the facility. However, here are some common daily tasks that a security manager may perform:

    o **Team Briefing:** The security manager starts the day by conducting a briefing with the security team. They communicate important information, such as any incidents or threats from the previous day, changes in procedures, or updates on security protocols. This helps ensure that the team is well-informed and prepared for their shifts.

    o **Patrols and Inspections:** The security manager may conduct regular patrols and inspections throughout the shopping centre. This involves monitoring areas for any signs of suspicious activities, checking security equipment (e.g., CCTV cameras, alarms), and identifying any potential security vulnerabilities or maintenance issues.

    o **Staff Scheduling:** The security manager is responsible for creating and managing the security team's work schedules. They ensure that all shifts are adequately staffed, taking into account peak hours, special events, and any other factors that may impact security needs.

    o **Incident Response:** If any security incidents occur during the day, the security manager takes charge of coordinating the response. They assess the situation, direct security personnel to the appropriate areas, and liaise with local law enforcement or emergency services if necessary. The security manager ensures that incidents are addressed promptly and effectively.

- o **Training and Development:** The security manager may allocate time for training sessions or professional development activities for the security team. This could include conducting training on new security procedures, providing updates on relevant laws or regulations, or organising refresher courses on emergency response or customer service skills.

- o **Documentation and Reporting:** The security manager maintains accurate records of security-related incidents, such as thefts, accidents, or disturbances. They ensure that incident reports are completed thoroughly and submitted on time. Additionally, the security manager may compile daily activity logs and other documentation related to security operations.

- o **Communication and Collaboration:** The security manager regularly communicates and collaborates with various stakeholders, including property owners, tenants, facility managers, and law enforcement agencies. They may attend meetings, respond to inquiries or concerns, and provide updates on security matters.

- o **Equipment and Supplies Management:** The security manager oversees the management of security equipment and supplies. This involves maintaining an inventory of security-related assets, ensuring their proper functioning, coordinating repairs or replacements, and ordering necessary supplies, such as uniforms, badges, or safety equipment.

- o **Emergency Preparedness:** The security manager continuously reviews and updates the shopping centre's emergency response plans. They may conduct drills or tabletop exercises to ensure that the security team is well-prepared to handle various emergency scenarios. The security manager also stays informed about any external threats or changes in the security landscape that may affect the shopping centre.

- **Customer Service:** In addition to their security responsibilities, the security manager may engage with shoppers and visitors to assist, answer questions, or address any security-related concerns. They strive to maintain a welcoming and safe environment for customers and enhance the overall shopping experience.

It's important to note that the daily chores of a security manager can be dynamic and may require flexibility to address unexpected incidents or changing priorities.

QUESTIONS AND ANSWERS SESSION - FM OPERATIONS

Q1: What is the role of MEP operations in shopping centres?

A1: MEP operations involve the maintenance, inspection, and management of mechanical, electrical, and plumbing systems in shopping centres to ensure their proper functioning and the comfort of tenants and visitors.

Q2: What are the responsibilities of shopping centre maintenance in MEP (Mechanical, Electrical, and Plumbing) operations?

2A: Shopping centre maintenance in MEP operations involves ensuring the proper functioning, maintenance, and inspection of mechanical systems (e.g., HVAC), electrical systems, plumbing systems, and other infrastructure-related components within the shopping centre.

Q3: What is common area maintenance in the context of shopping centres?

3A: Common area maintenance refers to the upkeep and maintenance of shared spaces within a shopping centre, such as corridors, parking lots, restrooms, escalators, and common seating areas. It ensures a clean, safe, and appealing environment for shoppers.

Q4: How can shopping centres implement energy-efficient practices in MEP operations?

4A: Shopping centres can implement energy-efficient practices in MEP operations by conducting energy audits, upgrading lighting systems, optimising HVAC systems, using smart building automation systems, promoting energy conservation awareness among tenants and staff, and investing in renewable energy sources.

Q5: What are some best practices for effective preventive maintenance in shopping centres?

5A: Some best practices for effective preventive maintenance in shopping centres include developing a comprehensive maintenance schedule, conducting regular inspections, implementing a computerised maintenance management system (CMMS), training staff on maintenance procedures, and prioritising proactive repairs and replacements.

Q6: How can technology and automation enhance security operations in shopping centres?

6A: Technology and automation can enhance security operations in shopping centres by implementing CCTV surveillance systems, access control systems, intrusion detection systems, video analytics, visitor management systems, remote monitoring, and incident reporting tools.

Q7: What strategies can shop centres employ to ensure a high standard of cleanliness and hygiene?

7A: Shopping centres can ensure a high standard of cleanliness and hygiene by employing well-trained and dedicated housekeeping staff, implementing regular cleaning schedules, using eco-friendly cleaning products, maintaining proper waste management systems, conducting inspections and audits, and engaging in continuous staff training.

Q8: How can shopping centres promote sustainable practices in facility management operations?

8A: Shopping centres can promote sustainable practices in facility management operations by implementing energy-efficient measures, reducing water consumption, practising waste reduction and recycling, using sustainable building materials, promoting green transportation options, and educating tenants and visitors about sustainable practices.

Q9: What is the importance of common area maintenance in shopping centres?

9A: Common area maintenance includes the upkeep and cleanliness of shared spaces within the shopping centre, ensuring a pleasant and safe environment for shoppers and tenants.

Q10: How can preventive maintenance contribute to the overall efficiency of a shopping centre?

10A: Preventive maintenance helps identify and address potential issues before they escalate, reducing the risk of equipment failure, improving energy efficiency, and minimising operational disruptions.

Q11; What is the difference between preventive maintenance and reactive maintenance?

11A: Preventive maintenance involves scheduled inspections and maintenance activities to prevent equipment failures, while reactive maintenance addresses issues after they occur.

Q12: How does housekeeping impact the overall experience of a shopping centre?

12A: Housekeeping operations, including cleaning protocols, floor care, and pest management, contribute to maintaining a clean, attractive, and hygienic shopping environment, enhancing the overall experience for shoppers.

Q13: What are some technological innovations revolutionising the housekeeping industry in shopping centres?

13A: Technological innovations such as automated cleaning systems, smart waste management, and IoT-enabled monitoring systems are revolutionising the housekeeping industry in shopping centres, improving efficiency and sustainability.

Q14: What are the important considerations in security operations within a shopping centre?

14A: Security operations in a shopping centre include activities such as access control, patrolling, car parking management, theft prevention, incident response, emergency procedures, and maintaining the safety and security of visitors, tenants, and property within the shopping centre.

Q15: How does security personnel contribute to theft prevention within retail stores in a shopping centre?

15A: Security personnel play a crucial role in preventing theft within retail stores by conducting regular patrols, monitoring surveillance systems, implementing access control measures, and responding promptly to suspicious activities or incidents.

Q16: Define Green Cleaning? & What are some examples of green cleaning measures implemented in shopping centres?

16A: Green cleaning or green housekeeping is an important aspect of sustainable practices, an evolving trend of today's times. This is a comparatively new concept, and the term is used for employing cleaning methods and products that are environment-friendly, i.e., which have ingredients and processes that inherently safeguard human health and the quality of the environment. Some examples of green cleaning measures in shopping centres include using environmentally friendly cleaning products, implementing waste management and recycling programmes, and promoting sustainable practices among staff and tenants.

Part 2 - FM Operations

Module 4

Details About Important MEP Systems

HVAC Systems In A Shopping Centre: Its Operations, Distribution, And Assembly

HVAC stands for Heating, Ventilation, and Air Conditioning. It is used to control and maintain indoor environmental conditions, including temperature, humidity, air quality, and airflow, in various buildings and spaces. Tenants, and employees. In a shopping centre, HVAC systems play a crucial role in providing comfort for shoppers, Key components of an HVAC system in a shopping centre include:

Key Components

- **Heating Equipment:**

    Furnace: A furnace is a device that generates heat, usually by burning fuel such as natural gas, oil, or propane. It provides warmth during colder periods.

- **Cooling Equipment:**

    Air Conditioner: An air conditioner cools the indoor air by removing heat and moisture from the space. It uses refrigeration principles to lower the temperature and maintain comfortable conditions.

Chiller: A chiller is a refrigeration machine that produces cold water or chilled air. It is commonly used in large shopping centres to cool the air and maintain a consistent temperature.

- Ventilation Equipment:

    Air Handling Unit (AHU): An AHU is responsible for distributing conditioned air throughout the shopping centre. It includes components such as fans, filters, and dampers to control the airflow and ensure proper ventilation.

    Exhaust Fans: Exhaust fans help remove stale air, doors, and contaminants from the building, improving indoor air quality.

- Ductwork:

    Supply Ducts: These are responsible for distributing conditioned air from the AHU to different areas of the shopping centre.

    Return Ducts: Return ducts collect the air from the spaces and transport it back to the AHU for treatment and reconditioning.

    Exhaust Ducts: Exhaust ducts remove air from specific areas, such as restrooms and kitchens, to maintain proper ventilation and prevent the spread of doors.

- Controls and Sensors:

    Thermostats: Thermostats regulate the temperature settings and provide control over heating and cooling systems.

    Humidity Sensors: These sensors monitor and control the humidity levels within the shopping centre to maintain a comfortable and healthy environment.

    CO2 Sensors: Carbon dioxide (CO_2) sensors detect the concentration of CO_2 in the air and help maintain adequate ventilation rates.

- **Air Filtration:**

  Air Filters: Air filters remove dust, pollen, pollutants, and other particles from the incoming air, improving indoor air quality and protecting the HVAC system from damage.

  These components work together to ensure proper heating, cooling, ventilation, and air quality control within the shopping centre, creating a comfortable and healthy environment for visitors and occupants.

Assembly Of Chillers And Chiller Yard

The assembly of chillers and the chiller yard refers to the arrangement and setup of the chiller units and associated equipment in a designated area known as the chiller yard. The chiller yard is where the chiller units, which are part of the HVAC system, are located and operated.

- **Chiller Units:**

  Chillers: These are large refrigeration machines that produce chilled water or cold air. They work by removing heat from the water or air, and cooling it down to the desired temperature.

  Compressors: Compressors are essential components of chillers that circulate refrigerant and compress it to increase its temperature and pressure.

  Condensers: Condensers facilitate the transfer of heat from the refrigerant to the outdoor air or cooling water, allowing the refrigerant to release the absorbed heat.

  Evaporators: Evaporators absorb heat from the chilled water or air, causing the refrigerant to evaporate and cool down the circulating medium.

  Expansion Devices: Expansion devices control the flow of refrigerant, reducing its pressure and temperature as it enters the evaporator.

- **Chiller Yard:**

    Location: The chiller yard is usually an outdoor area designated for the installation of chillers and associated equipment. It is typically located adjacent to the shopping centre building or on the rooftop, depending on the available space and design considerations.

    Foundations and Supports: The chillers are mounted on concrete foundations or support structures to provide stability and minimise vibrations.

    Piping Systems: Various pipes, including supply and return lines, connect the chillers to the rest of the HVAC system within the shopping centre.

    Electrical Connections: Electrical cables and connections are installed to provide power supply to the chillers and associated equipment.

    Control Systems: Control panels, sensors, and automation systems are implemented to monitor and regulate the operation of the chillers, ensuring efficient and optimal performance.

    Cooling Towers: Cooling towers would be installed on the rooftop or an outdoor area to dissipate heat from the chiller system. They use evaporation to cool down the condenser water from the chillers.

Safety and Security

Safety measures such as fencing, barriers, and warning signs may be in place to protect the chiller yard and equipment from unauthorised access and ensure a safe working environment.

<u>The assembly of chillers and the chiller yard is crucial for the effective operation of the HVAC system in the shopping centre. It allows for centralised cooling and temperature control, ensuring a comfortable environment for shoppers, tenants, and employees. Proper installation, maintenance, and regular inspections of the chiller units and chiller yard are essential to maximise the efficiency, reliability, and longevity of the HVAC system.</u>

- Within the HVAC (Heating, Ventilation, and Air Conditioning) system, FCUs, AHUs, and FAHUs are commonly used components.

Here's a breakdown of each of these components and their assemblies:

FCU (Fan Coil Unit):

Definition: An FCU is a device that consists of a coil, fan, and filters. It is typically installed within individual spaces or zones of a building to provide localised heating and cooling.

Assembly:

Coil: The coil within an FCU contains chilled water or hot water, depending on the desired cooling or heating mode. It transfers heat between the air passing over it and the water circulating through the coil.

Fan: The fan in an FCU blows air across the coil, facilitating the heat exchange process and distributing conditioned air into the space.

Filters: Filters are incorporated within the FCU to remove dust, particles, and other impurities from the air before it enters the space.

- **AHU (Air Handling Unit):**

    Definition: An AHU is a large assembly that conditions and distributes air throughout a building. It is responsible for supplying fresh air, as well as heating and cooling.

Assembly:

Housing: The AHU is contained within a housing that encloses the various components.

Fans: Multiple fans are present in an AHU, including supply fans that push conditioned air into the building and exhaust fans that remove stale air from the building.

Heat Exchangers: Heat exchangers, such as coils or plates, transfer heat between the air and a fluid medium, such as chilled water or hot water, to achieve cooling or heating.

Filters: Air filters are installed to remove dust, allergens, and other particles from the air before it is distributed.

Humidifier/Dehumidifier: In some AHUs, humidifiers or dehumidifiers are included to control the humidity levels in the air.

Dampers: Dampers regulate the flow of air within the AHU, allowing for control of the airflow rate and distribution.

Controls: Control systems and sensors manage the operation of the AHU, ensuring optimal performance and maintaining desired environmental conditions.

- **FAHU (Fresh Air Handling Unit):**

    Definition: A FAHU is a specialised type of AHU designed to specifically handle fresh air intake, filtration, and distribution in a building.

Assembly:

Similar to an AHU, a FAHU incorporates many of the same components, such as fans, filters, heat exchangers, dampers, and controls. The key distinction is that an FAHU is primarily dedicated to handling the intake and treatment of fresh air from the external environment, which is then supplied to the building's spaces.

These components, FCUs, AHUs, and FAHUs, are integral parts of HVAC systems and play crucial roles in providing heating, cooling, ventilation, and air quality control in commercial buildings like shopping centres. Their assemblies are designed to optimise the performance, energy efficiency, and comfort of the indoor environment.

- Water Source in Chillers and Cooling Tower

    The water used in chillers and cooling towers in a shopping centre's HVAC system typically comes from two different sources:

- Chilled Water in Chillers:

    Makeup Water: For chillers that use a water-cooled system, makeup water is supplied to the chiller plant. This makeup water is sourced from the building's water supply or a dedicated water source such as a well or water storage tanks.

    Water Treatment: Before entering the chiller system, the makeup water goes through a water treatment process to ensure it meets the required quality standards. Water treatment may involve filtration, chemical treatment, and disinfection to remove impurities, control scaling, and prevent corrosion.

- Condenser Water in Cooling Towers:

    Circulating Water: Cooling towers use circulating water for heat dissipation. The circulating water is typically sourced from the chiller plant's condenser water loop.

    Closed Loop: The condenser water loop forms a closed system, continuously circulating water between the chillers and the cooling towers.

    Evaporation and Makeup: As the condenser water flows through the cooling towers, a portion of it evaporates to facilitate heat transfer. To maintain the desired water levels, makeup water is added to the condenser water loop from a separate water supply source.

    Water Treatment: Similar to makeup water for chillers, the makeup water for the condenser water loop also undergoes water treatment to ensure its quality and prevent scaling, fouling, and corrosion.

Both chilled water and condenser water are integral to the operation of the HVAC system in a shopping centre. Proper water treatment and monitoring are essential to maintain system efficiency, prevent equipment damage, and ensure a reliable and consistent cooling process. Water management practices, including filtration, chemical treatment, and regular maintenance, are implemented to optimise the performance and lifespan of the chillers and cooling towers.

Mechanical Equipment in a Shopping Centre

- HVAC Systems:

    Chillers, cooling towers, air handling units (AHUs), fan coil units (FCUs), ductwork, fans, and ventilation systems.

- Plumbing and Water Supply:

    Water pumps, water storage tanks, water treatment systems, piping network, water fixtures (sinks, faucets, toilets), and drainage systems.

- Fire Protection:

    Fire pumps, fire hydrants, sprinkler systems, fire hoses, fire extinguishers, and fire suppression systems.

- Elevators and Escalators:

    Elevators, escalators, and moving walkways for vertical transportation within the shopping centre.

Electrical Equipment in a Shopping Centre:

- Electrical Distribution:

    Transformers, switchgear, distribution panels, circuit breakers, and electrical cables.

- **Lighting Systems:**

  Interior and exterior lighting fixtures, emergency lighting systems, and lighting controls.

- **Power Supply and Backup:**

  Electrical generators, uninterruptible power supply (UPS) systems, and backup power distribution.

- **Security Systems:**

  CCTV cameras, access control systems, intrusion detection systems, and alarm systems.

Module 5

BMS (Building Management System) In A Shopping Centre

A Building Management System (BMS) in shopping centre's is a centralised control system that monitors and manages various building systems and processes, such as HVAC (heating, ventilation, and air conditioning), lighting, security, and energy usage.

Assembly

Control panels, sensors, and actuators for HVAC control, lighting control, energy management, and monitoring of various building parameters.

Advantages of implementing a BMS in shopping centres include:

- **Energy Efficiency:** BMS helps optimise energy usage by controlling and automating various systems based on occupancy, temperature, and other factors. This can result in significant energy savings and cost reduction.

- **Improved Comfort and Environment:** BMS ensures optimal temperature, ventilation, and lighting conditions throughout the shopping centre, enhancing the comfort of visitors and occupants. It also helps maintain indoor air quality and provides a pleasant shopping experience.

- **Centralised Control and Monitoring:** BMS provides a centralised platform to monitor and control various building systems. It allows facility managers to efficiently manage and maintain equipment, detect and resolve issues, and respond quickly to emergencies.

- **Data Analysis and Insights:** BMS collects and analyses data from different building systems, providing valuable insights into energy consumption patterns, equipment performance, and maintenance needs. This information can help optimise operations, plan maintenance schedules, and make informed decisions for future improvements.

- **Enhanced Security:** BMS integrates with security systems, including access control and surveillance, to monitor and manage the safety of the shopping centre. It enables proactive security measures, such as alarms, notifications, and remote monitoring, to prevent and respond to incidents effectively.

- **Cost Savings:** By optimising energy usage, improving maintenance efficiency, and reducing equipment downtime, BMS can lead to significant cost savings over time.

It helps minimise operational expenses, extend equipment lifespans, and reduce the need for manual interventions.

Overall, a BMS in shopping centres offers centralised control, energy efficiency, improved comfort, enhanced security, and cost savings, contributing to a more sustainable, efficient, and enjoyable shopping environment.

Fire Suppression Equipment in a Shopping Centre

- Sprinkler Systems:

    Water sprinklers were installed throughout the shopping centre to suppress fires by releasing water when triggered by heat.

- Fire Alarm Systems:

    Smoke detectors, heat detectors, manual call points, and control panels to detect and alert occupants in case of fire.

- Fire Extinguishers:

    Portable fire extinguishers placed at strategic locations for immediate fire suppression.

M. Nauman Thakur

FM 2000 And Where It Is Used In Shopping Centres

FM-200 (Heptafluoropropane) is a clean gaseous fire suppression agent that is commonly used in various settings, including shopping centres, to protect against fire hazards. FM200 is an effective and environmentally friendly fire suppression solution that is designed to extinguish fires quickly without causing damage to sensitive equipment or leaving behind residue. Here are some areas within a shopping centre where FM-200 may be used:

Data Centres: Shopping centres often have data centres or server rooms that house critical IT infrastructure. FM-200 can be installed in these areas to protect valuable equipment and quickly suppress fires that may occur.

- **Electrical Equipment Rooms:** FM-200 can be used to protect electrical equipment rooms, such as switchgear rooms, UPS rooms, and electrical distribution areas, where fires involving electrical components can pose significant risks.

- **Control Rooms:** Control rooms that house monitoring and control systems, including HVAC control systems, fire alarm panels, and security systems, can be safeguarded with FM-200 to prevent fire damage.

- **Storage Areas:** Shopping centres typically have storage areas where goods, inventory, or combustible materials are stored. FM-200 can be utilised in these areas to provide fire protection and minimise the potential damage caused by fire.

  Mechanical Rooms: FM-200 can be deployed in mechanical rooms that house HVAC equipment, pumps, and other mechanical systems to mitigate fire risks and protect these critical components.

- <u>Define Isolator, SMDBs, MDBsand their mechanism</u>

  In an electrical room, various components and equipment are installed to distribute electrical power to different areas of a building or facility. Here are the definitions of some common distribution panels used in electrical rooms:

Isolator:

An isolator, also known as an isolating switch or disconnect switch, is a manually operated switch used to isolate an electrical circuit from the power source. It allows for safe maintenance or repair work on the electrical system by completely disconnecting the power supply.

SMDB (Sub-Main Distribution Board):

A Sub-Main Distribution Board is a panel that receives power from the main distribution board and distributes it to various sub-circuits or sub-panels within a building. It typically contains circuit breakers or fuses to protect the sub-circuits from overloads or short circuits. SMDBs are usually located closer to the loads they serve, such as on different floors or areas of the building.

MDB (Main Distribution Board):

The Main Distribution Board, also known as the Main Switchboard or Main Panel, is the primary distribution point for electrical power entering a building. It receives power from the electrical utility or a backup power source and distributes it to various sub-circuits through circuit breakers or fuses. MDBs often house protective devices, such as surge protectors, main circuit breakers, and power monitoring equipment.

MCC (Motor Control Centre):

A Motor Control Centre is a specialised distribution panel that provides centralised control and protection for electrical motors and motor-driven equipment. It contains motor starters, overload relays, control devices, and circuit breakers designed specifically for motor control applications. MCCs are commonly used in large commercial or industrial facilities with numerous motors.

These distribution panels play crucial roles in safely and efficiently distributing electrical power throughout a building or facility. They help regulate and protect the electrical circuits, allowing for proper control, isolation, and distribution of power to different loads.

The specific configuration and components within these panels may vary depending on the building's electrical requirements, local regulations, and the size of the electrical distribution system. It's important to consult with electrical engineers and adhere to relevant codes and standards when designing and installing distribution panels in electrical rooms.

Load Distribution of the HV Transfer in a Shopping Centre

In a shopping centre, the electrical load is typically divided into various categories based on the nature of the load. These categories may include lighting, HVAC systems, escalators/elevators, common areas, tenant spaces, and other auxiliary loads. The load distribution for the major HV transformer would depend on factors such as the size of the transformer, the capacity of the HT transformers, and the overall electrical load demand of the shopping centre.

A common approach is to have a centralised electrical distribution system with the major HV transformer supplying power to HT transformers, which in turn distribute power to different sections or zones of the shopping centre. The load distribution may be managed through electrical switchgear, panel boards, and distribution boards.

Here's a general example of load distribution for a major HV transformer in a shopping centre:

Lighting: The major HV transformer would supply power to dedicated HT transformers that distribute electricity to the lighting fixtures throughout the shopping centre, including common areas, corridors, parking lots, and other illuminated spaces.

HVAC Systems: Another set of HT transformers would be responsible for supplying power to the HVAC systems, including chillers, AHUs, and fans. These transformers would distribute power to the mechanical rooms and air conditioning units throughout the shopping centre.

Escalators/Elevators: HT transformers specifically dedicated to escalators and elevators would supply power to these systems, ensuring smooth operation and reliable transportation within the shopping centre.

Tenant Spaces: HT transformers allocated for tenant spaces would distribute power to individual shops, stores, and other leased areas within the shopping centre, allowing tenants to meet their specific electrical requirements.

Common Areas: Dedicated HT transformers would supply power to common areas such as food courts, atriums, lobbies, and public spaces within the shopping centre.

Auxiliary Loads: Additional HT transformers may be assigned to support auxiliary loads such as water pumps, fire protection systems, security systems, and other specialised electrical equipment.

DG Set (Diesel Generator Set):

A DG set is an independent power generation unit typically fuelled by diesel. It serves as a backup or alternative power source when the primary electrical supply from the grid fails or during periods of high electricity demand. DG sets are commonly used in shopping malls to ensure continuous power supply for critical systems, such as emergency lighting, fire alarm systems, elevators, and other essential equipment, during power outages.

Carbon Emission Vents:

In a shopping mall, carbon emission vents are part of the mechanical ventilation system. These vents are designed to expel exhaust gases, including carbon dioxide (CO_2) and other emissions produced by combustion processes, such as those generated by DG sets or other fuel-burning equipment. The carbon emission vents help maintain good indoor air quality by removing pollutants and maintaining a healthy environment within the mall.

Proper maintenance, ventilation design, and emission control measures should be implemented to minimise the environmental impact and ensure compliance with applicable regulations.

Appendix

A3

Certain items in a shopping center should be checked daily, usually before the mall is opened, by maintenance or other personnel. Any deficiencies should be reported immediately to management. The extent of the items to be checked daily will vary from center to center.

Daily Maintenance Checklist

Date of Inspection:_____

Any Deficiencies Must Be Reported to Management Immediately

Item	Checked By	Location and Action Taken
Mall Lights		
Tenant Signage		
Traffic Signage		
Common Area HVAC		
Mall Entrance/Exits		
Awnings		
Exterior Store Floodlights		
Mall Floors		
Unauthorized Items in Common Area		
Music System		
Service Areas		
Interior Store Lights		
Rest Rooms		
Drinking Fountains		
Locks		
Freight Loading Areas		
Compactor		
Elevators/Escalators		
Parking Lot/Garage		
Other_____		
Other_____		
Other_____		

Inspected by:_____

Shopping Centre Management - FM Operations

A5 | This report records the condition of the equipment to insure satisfactory performance and/or indicate replacement. It also serves as evidence of due diligence in the event of fire and as an inventory control form. Similar forms should be used by tenants for their own fire extinguishers. A plan of the building should be attached, noting the location of each fire extinguisher.

Monthly Fire Extinguisher Inspection

Location of Extinguisher	Type	Serial No.	Comments/Action Taken or Necessary

Location of Pull Stations	Comments/Action Taken or Necessary

Inspected by:_____ Date of Inspection:_____

A6	This inspection checklist is generally used in large centers as an extension of periodic fire prevention inspections. An annunciator plan should be attached. Similar inspections should be made of the annunciator panel, smoke detectors, sprinkler systems, and stairwell pressurization.

Supervised Fire Line Valve and Road Box Inspection

Valve Number	Location	Open	Shut	Sealed	Controls	Water Pressure	Road Box

Date of Inspection:_____   Inspected by:_____

Shopping Centre Management - FM Operations

A9 Inspections of escalators and moving stairways are usually made by service companies familiar with the equipment and responsible for its upkeep. One copy of their regular inspection findings, as recorded on this form, is provided to center management for its files and as documentation that the equipment is performing safely and efficiently.

Escalator Inspection Report Form

Route No._____ Store_____ Date_____ Division_____

Mechanical Equipment Inspection

Component	Condition	Adjustment	Lubrication	Cleaning	Repair/Replace
Motor Bearings					
Main Drive Chain					
Step Chains and Steps					
Comb Plates					
Hand Rail					
Hand Rail Drive Chain					
Tension Carriage Bearings					
Main Bearing, Upper Drive					
Step Wheel and Bearing					
Tension Carriage Rollers					
Lower Newel Bearing					
Access Panel and Doors					

Escalator Inspection

Device	Condition	Adjustment	Cleaning	Repair/Replace
Motor Brake				
Brake-Operated Switch				
Fire Door Contact Switch				
Broken Drive Chain Contact				
Friction Reversal Device				
Left Broken Step Chain Contact				
Right Broken Step Chain Contact				
Drive Motor				
Stop Button, Upper Landing				
Stop Button, Lower Landing				
Starting Switch, Upper Landing				
Starting Switch, Lower Landing				
S.V.C. Thermal Overload Circuit Breaker				
Left Step and Skirt Safety Switch				
Right Step and Skirt Safety Switch				
Service Cutout Switch				

Equipment Cleaning and Housekeeping

Oil Drip Pan	
Pits and Drains	
Motor Pit	

Control Panel Electrical

Contacts	
Coils	
Flexible Leads	
Lugs and Posts	

Remarks_____ Inspectors_____

B6 — Emergency generating equipment must be regularly maintained and periodically run in accordance with manufacturers' recommendations to assure that it will function when called upon. This form records pertinent data. Attach a list of the equipment it will operate in an emergency, as well as a plan of the shopping center indicating the areas that the generator services.

Emergency Generator Operation Log

Name of Operator_____   Date_____
Time Start_____   Time Stop_____
Reverse Polarity_____

Engine

Vacuum Reading	_____	Batteries:	☐ OK ☐ Need Changing ☐ Need Replacement
Gasoline Supply	_____ gals.		Oil Filter Condition _____
Oil Supply	_____ qts.		
Antifreeze	_____ qts.		Water Level _____ _____ gals.

Comments

_____
_____
_____
_____
_____
_____
_____
_____
_____
_____

Shopping Centre Management - FM Operations

J5

This checklist is used to call the maintenance department's attention to a wide variety of physical problems in the center itself as well as in the common areas. Problems requiring immediate attention would be communicated to maintenance in a less formal manner.

Maintenance Checklist

To: Superintendent Of Maintenance
From: Security Department
Subject: Traffic Safety, Miscellaneous Condition

At the location(s) indicated, the condition(s) indicated by 'X' exist(s). It is recommended that appropriate action be taken to remedy such condition(s).
Location: _____

☐ Stop Signs	☐ Broken	☐ Defaced	☐ Need Painting
☐ Speed Limit Signs	☐ Broken	☐ Defaced	☐ Need Painting
☐ One Way Street Signs	☐ Broken	☐ Defaced	☐ Need Painting
☐ Parking Signs	☐ Broken	☐ Defaced	☐ Need Painting

☐ Directional Arrows and/or Markers Need Repainting
☐ Crosswalks Need Repainting
☐ Stop Signs Needed Due To   ☐ Blind Corner   ☐ Heavy One-Way Traffic
☐ Crosswalk Needed Due To Heavy Pedestrian Traffic
☐ Traffic Lights   ☐ Defective   ☐ Out Of Order
☐ Curb Markings Need Repainting
☐ Restricted Parking Signs Needed
☐ Tree Branches Obstructing Signs, Hazardous Conditions
☐ Plumbing Fixtures, Faucets, Leakage, etc.
☐ Lights - Parking Area - Corridor, Concourse
☐ Lights - Tenants' Signs
☐ Rubbish Accumulated
☐ Dust Accumulated
☐ Restrooms (Vandalism)
☐ Escalator Conditions
☐ Condition of Vehicles, Scooters, Trucks, Hi-Lift
☐ Other Problems (Explain in Detail) _____

Remarks (Show Location and Action Taken or Recommended) _____

Signed _____
Date _____   Time _____

A1

Lighting inspections should be made nightly, and action should be taken as quickly as possible to correct an unsatisfactory situation. Use a parking lot plan and number each lamp on it for easy reference. Use the reverse side to record results of the nightly check of stores.

Nightly Lighting Report

Location	Hour Checked	Nature of Problem	Action Taken
Ramp Lights			
Signs			
Parking Area			
Roof Lights			
Entrance/Exit Lights			
Photo Cells/Timers			
Emergency Lights			
Loading Docks			
Service Aisles			
Other			

Shopping Centre Management - FM Operations

Inspection of Common Areas and Building Exteriors

Property_____
Inspected By_____   Date_____
Time_____   Weather Condition_____

Area Inspected	Condition		Remarks
	Satisfactory	Unsatisfactory	
Common Area			
Blacktop			
Parking Area			
Entrances			
Driveways			
Curbs			
Signs			
Speed Limit			
Traffic Control			
Handicapped Signs			
Lot Striping			
Parking Spaces			
Stop Bars			
Lane Markers			
Cross Walks			
Curbs			
Landscaping			
Grass			
Shrubs			
Trees			
Electrical			
Canopy Lights			
Pole Condition			
Pole Lights			
Security Lights			
Set Time Clocks			
Sewers			
Storm Catch Basins			
Sanitary Manholes			
Fire Hydrants			
Maintenance			
Lot Cleanliness			
Bass Cart Control			
Abandoned Cars			
Unauthorized Vendors			
Rear Trash			

Inspection of Common Areas and Building Exteriors   Page 2

Area Inspected	Condition		Remarks
	Satisfactory	Unsatisfactory	

J8   This form is helpful in detailing any offenses committed on the center property, even those resolved by center security without assistance from local police. Properly filed, it also can serve as a continuing reference on 'regular' troublemakers.

Report of Offense on Property

Case Number _____
Date of Report _____

Print Name	
Age _____ Date of Birth _____	
Address _____ City _____ Phone _____	
Weight ____ Height ____ Eyes ____ Hair ____ Complexion ____	
Employed at _____ (Or School) _____	
Employer's Business Address _____ School Grade ____	
Position Held	

If Juvenile, Fill In Below:

Father's Name _____	Mother's Name _____
Address _____	Address _____
City _____	City _____
State _____	State _____
Phone _____	Phone _____

Officer to Fill in Below

Date of Disturbance _____ Time of Disturbance _____ Place _____
Offense Charged With _____

Description of Disturbance (Include Property Involved) _____
If Previous Violation, State Where _____
Attitude of Suspect While Being Held _____

Action Taken By This Department _____

Officer in Charge Of Questioning
I, _____ do swear that the above statements given are the truth to the best of my knowledge.

Signed _____
(Security Officer)

Shopping Centre Management - FM Operations

J11 — This page shows two types of forms used for parking violations. The form on the left warns of parking violations within the center. In cases of serious violations the car may be towed away. The form is perforated so that the stub on the right can be retained to keep a record of repeat offenders. The form on the right is a notice that is placed on car windshields. The security officer keeps a record of these offenses. (See Forms J1 and J2)

Parking Violation Notices

Vehicle _____	License _____
Date _____	Time _____

WARNING

You have violated Traffic Regulations as indicated:
1. Improperly Parked in Stall ☐
2. Parked in Roadway ☐
3. Parked in Handicapped Zone ☐
4. Blocking Traffic ☐
5. Parked in Truck Dock ☐
6. Employee in Customer Area ☐

In the interest of safety and convenience your cooperation is invited in observing regulations on reverse side.

Front

| Violation No. _____ |
| Type _____ |
| Time _____ |
| Date _____ |
| Location _____ |
| License Tag # _____ |
| Make _____ |
| Color _____ |
| Officer _____ |

The Center has been planned for shopping ease to provide safe and convenient parking all the following regulations must be observed.

Traffic Regulations
- Obey Stop and Yield Signs
- Obey Directional Arrows
- Obey Speed Signs

Parking Regulations
- Park Cars Nose-in to Center of Stall
- No Parking Along Curbs
- No Parking in Painted Crosshatch Markings

Safety Regulations
- Drive Carefully - Be Alert
- Hand Brake on Tightly When Parked
- Observe Courtesy of the Road

Back

THIS VEHICLE IS IMPROPERLY PARKED

CENTER REGULATIONS STATE THAT IMPROPERLY PARKED VEHICLES MAY BE SUBJECT TO BEING TOWED AWAY AT THE OWNER'S EXPENSE. THIS VEHICLE IS IMPROPERLY PARKED:

☐ BLOCKING FIRE LANE   ☐ IN LOADING ZONE
☐ BLOCKING BUILDING ENTRANCE ☐ IN THE HANDICAPPED ZONE
☐ OTHER _____

YOUR LICENSE TAG NUMBER HAS BEEN RECORDED AND REPEATED VIOLATIONS WILL CAUSE YOUR VEHICLE TO BE REMOVED.

Glossary

FM Operations

1. HVAC Systems: Heating, Ventilation, and Air Conditioning systems that regulate the indoor climate of a shopping centre, ensuring comfort and air quality for visitors and tenants.

2. BMS (Building Management System): An integrated system that monitors and controls various building functions, including HVAC, lighting, security, and fire safety, for efficient and centralized management.

3. Housekeeping Operations: The department responsible for maintaining the cleanliness and upkeep of common areas, restrooms, and other public spaces within the shopping centre.

4. Security Operations: The department responsible for ensuring the safety and security of visitors, tenants, and assets within the shopping centre premises.

These definitions provide a foundational understanding of key terms and concepts used throughout the handbook, enabling professionals in shopping centre management to navigate the content effectively and make informed decisions.

This Handbook is designed to provide a helpful and informative overview of the topics covered. it is not intended to be a substitute for more extensive learning that can be achieved through attending ICSC educational programs and reading additional ICSC professional publications.

You Write. We Publish.

To publish your own book, contact us.

We publish poetry collections, short story collections, novellas and novels.

contact@thewriteorder.com

Instagram- thewriteorder

www.facebook.com/thewriteorder

Shopping Centre Management - H.S.E Practices

M. Nauman Thakur

Contents

H.S.E Practises In A Shopping Centre	1
• Safety Training and Awareness	5
• Questions And Answers Session - HSE Practices In Shopping Centres	7
Shopping Centre Management - Construction Document	9
• Professional Project Delivery in Shopping Centre Management	8
• Advantages of Stakeholder Protection in Shopping Centre Management	10
Construction: Introduction	11
• Pre-Construction Phase	15
• MEP and Civil Works	17
• Construction Phase	18
• Project Completion and Handover	19
• Checklist for MEP Testing and Commissioning	22
• Post-Construction Stage	25
• HVAC Testing and Commissioning Checklist	27
• Electrical Systems Testing and Commissioning Checklist	28
• Plumbing and Sanitary Systems Testing and Commissioning Checklist	29
• Fire and Life Safety Systems Testing and Commissioning Checklist	29
• Elevator and Escalator Testing and Commissioning Checklist	30
• Defect Liability Period	30
• Purpose of the Defect Liability Period:	31
• Defect Liability Protocol	31
• Mitigating Delays and Protecting Stakeholders' Equity	32

Introduction To Shopping Centre Operational Metrics   35
- Shopping Centre Metrics   43
- Key Shopping Centre Operational Metrics   35
- Benefits of Tracking Occupancy Rate   36
- Using Shopping Centre Operational Metrics   38
- Challenges and Considerations   39
- Key Takeaways   40
- Questions And Answers Session - Metrics   40

Glossary   41
- HSE and Its Practices   41
- Shopping Centre Metrics   41

H.S.E Practises In A Shopping Centre

HSE stands for Health, Safety, and Environment. It refers to a set of practices, policies, and regulations aimed at ensuring the well-being, protection, and sustainability of individuals and the environment within various settings, including shopping centres.

HSE is crucial in shopping centres for the following reasons:

- **Customer Safety:**

    Shopping centres attract large numbers of people, and ensuring their safety is of paramount importance. HSE measures help prevent accidents, injuries, and other incidents that could harm shoppers. This includes maintaining clean and well-lit spaces, managing crowd control, and implementing proper signage for emergency exits and hazards.

- **Employee Safety:**

    Shopping centres have a significant workforce, including retail staff, security personnel, maintenance workers, and others. HSE guidelines safeguard the well-being of employees by providing training on occupational hazards, promoting ergonomic practices, and enforcing safety protocols to prevent workplace accidents.

- **Risk Management:**

    Implementing effective HSE practices helps shopping centres identify potential risks and develop strategies to mitigate them. This includes conducting regular risk assessments, maintaining fire safety measures, ensuring proper handling and storage of hazardous materials, and addressing potential security threats.

- Risk Assessment:

It involves identifying, evaluating, and prioritising potential risks and hazards within a specific environment or activity. In the context of shopping centres, risk assessments are conducted to understand the potential risks to customers, employees, and the environment and to develop appropriate control measures to mitigate those risks.

Here are some key aspects of risk assessment in HSE:

- Hazard Identification:

The first step in risk assessment is identifying potential hazards that could cause harm or damage. In a shopping centre, hazards can include slip and trip hazards, fire risks, electrical hazards, unsafe equipment or fixtures, security vulnerabilities, or environmental concerns.

- Risk Evaluation:

Once hazards are identified, a thorough evaluation is conducted to determine the likelihood and severity of potential harm or damage. This involves assessing factors such as the frequency of exposure, the potential consequences, and the vulnerability of individuals or assets.

- Risk Prioritisation:

Risks are then prioritised based on their significance, allowing resources to be allocated effectively. Risks with higher severity or likelihood may be given higher priority for immediate attention and mitigation.

- Control Measures:

After identifying and prioritising risks, control measures are implemented to reduce or eliminate the identified hazards. These measures can include engineering controls (e.g., installing safety barriers), administrative controls (e.g., implementing safety procedures and policies), and personal protective equipment (PPE) requirements.

- **Monitoring and Review:**

  Risk assessments should be periodically reviewed and updated to account for changes in the shopping centre's operations, layout, or regulations. Regular monitoring is necessary to ensure that control measures remain effective and that new hazards are promptly identified and addressed.

- **Documentation and Communication:**

  Proper documentation of the risk assessment process, including hazard identification, risk evaluation, and control measures, is essential for record-keeping and regulatory compliance. It is also crucial to communicate the identified risks and control measures to employees, stakeholders, and relevant authorities to ensure awareness and cooperation in maintaining a safe environment. By conducting thorough risk assessments, shopping centres can proactively identify potential hazards, prioritise their management, and implement appropriate control measures.

  <u>This helps to reduce the likelihood of accidents, injuries, and incidents, enhancing the overall safety and well-being of customers, employees, and the environment.</u>

- **Environmental Management:**

  Implementing environmentally sustainable practices, such as waste management, energy efficiency measures, and water conservation initiatives, reduces the shopping centre's environmental impact. Promoting recycling programmes and providing designated recycling bins encourages shoppers and tenants to participate in waste reduction efforts.

  Raising awareness about environmental responsibility and encouraging sustainability initiatives among tenants and visitors fosters a culture of environmental consciousness.

- **Environmental Sustainability:**

    Shopping centres can have a significant environmental impact due to their energy consumption, waste generation, and carbon emissions. Incorporating environmental considerations into HSE practices promotes sustainable operations, including energy-efficient lighting, waste management systems, recycling programs, and environmentally friendly construction and renovation methods.

- **Reputation and Customer Satisfaction:**

    By prioritising HSE measures, shopping centres create a safer and more pleasant environment for customers. This enhances their reputation and fosters customer loyalty and satisfaction. Shoppers are more likely to frequent establishments that prioritise their safety and well-being.

    Overall, HSE is essential in shopping centres to protect the health and safety of customers, employees, and the environment, manage risks, ensure compliance with regulations, and enhance the overall shopping experience.

Other key features that are equally of significance related to the safety of shopping centres

- **Emergency Preparedness and Response:**

    Establishing emergency response procedures and protocols, including evacuation plans, fire safety measures, and emergency contact information, ensures a coordinated and efficient response during emergencies.

- Conducting regular drills and exercises helps familiarise staff with emergency procedures and enhances their ability to respond effectively in real-life situations.

- Maintaining clear and visible signage throughout the shopping centre ensures that customers and employees can easily locate emergency exits, assembly points, and emergency contact numbers.

Safety Training and Awareness

Providing comprehensive safety training to employees, contractors, and tenants within the shopping centre ensures they are equipped with the knowledge and skills to work safely.

- Training staff on emergency response procedures, equipment handling, proper use of personal protective equipment (PPE), and safety protocols reduces the risk of accidents and injuries. Promoting a safety-conscious culture encourages employees to actively report hazards, near misses, or incidents, fostering continuous improvement in safety practices.

- Maintenance and Inspections:

  Regular inspections of facilities, equipment, and infrastructure help identify potential safety hazards or maintenance issues that could pose risks. Routine maintenance, repair, and replacement of equipment ensures its proper functioning and minimises the likelihood of accidents. Assessing the condition of walkways, staircases, escalators, elevators, and other common areas helps identify and rectify any potential trip hazards or malfunctioning equipment.

- Fire Safety:

  Installing and maintaining fire detection and suppression systems, such as alarms, smoke detectors, fire extinguishers, and sprinkler systems, throughout the shopping centre reduces the risk of fire-related incidents.

  - Conducting periodic fire drills educates and prepares employees and tenants on evacuation procedures and safe assembly points in case of a fire.

  - Regular inspection and testing of fire safety equipment ensure their reliability and compliance with safety regulations.

- **Security and Crime Prevention:**

    Implementing security measures like CCTV surveillance systems, security personnel, access control systems, and well-lit areas deters criminal activities and enhances the safety of shoppers and employees. Establishing procedures for handling incidents such as theft, vandalism, or disruptive behaviour ensures a swift and appropriate response and collaboration with law enforcement authorities when required. Providing training to security staff on conflict resolution, crowd management, and emergency response equips them with the necessary.

- **Regular Audits and Continuous Improvement:**

    Conducting regular audits and inspections helps assess the effectiveness of HSE practices and identify areas for improvement. Engaging with stakeholders, including employees, tenants, and shoppers, allows for gathering feedback and suggestions to enhance safety and environmental measures.

- **Legal Compliance:**

    Shopping centres are subject to various health, safety, and environmental regulations imposed by local, regional, and national authorities. Compliance with these regulations is necessary to avoid legal issues, penalties, and reputational damage. HSE practices help shopping centres meet these compliance requirements and demonstrate a commitment to the well-being of their stakeholders.

    By implementing and maintaining robust HSE practices, shopping centres can ensure the well-being of all stakeholders, enhance customer satisfaction, minimise risks, and create a safe, secure, and sustainable shopping environment.

QUESTIONS AND ANSWERS SESSION - HSE PRACTICES IN SHOPPING CENTRES

Q1: What are the key components of an emergency management plan for shopping centres?

A1: The key components of an emergency management plan for shopping centres include emergency response procedures, evacuation plans, communication protocols, emergency contacts and resources, training and drills, coordination with local authorities, and post-incident recovery plans.

Q2: How can shopping centres effectively communicate safety procedures to tenants and visitors?

A2: Shopping centres can effectively communicate safety procedures to tenants and visitors by displaying clear signage, providing safety information on their website and mobile apps, conducting safety orientation sessions for tenants, organising safety awareness campaigns, and maintaining open lines of communication with tenants and visitors.

Q3: What measures can be implemented to prevent and manage incidents of theft and security breaches in shopping centres?

A3: Measures to prevent and manage incidents of theft and security breaches in shopping centres include implementing surveillance systems, training security personnel, conducting regular patrols and inspections, ensuring proper access control, installing alarm systems, collaborating with local law enforcement, and fostering a safe and secure environment.

Q4: How can shopping centres engage with the local community to promote safety and environmental awareness?

A4: Shopping centres can engage with the local community to promote safety and environmental awareness by organising safety and environmental awareness campaigns, partnering with local organisations and authorities, hosting community events and workshops, supporting local sustainability initiatives, and actively seeking feedback and suggestions from the community.

Shopping Centre Management - H.S.E Practices

> **Q5:** What are some examples of successful HSE practices implemented by leading shopping centres?
>
> **A5:** Some examples of successful HSE practices implemented by leading shopping centres include implementing comprehensive emergency response plans, conducting regular safety and evacuation drills, employing advanced security systems and trained personnel, implementing sustainable building designs and operations, promoting energy and water conservation, and actively engaging with the local community on safety and environmental initiatives.

Shopping Centre Management - Construction Document

(Guidelines - Project Delivery and Stakeholder Protection)

Brief: As shopping centre's serve as bustling hubs of commercial activity, the effective execution of projects within these spaces directly impacts their overall success and reputation. Simultaneously, safeguarding the interests of diverse stakeholders, including retailers, customers, investors, employees, and the surrounding community, is imperative to foster trust, loyalty, and sustainable growth. In this dynamic and competitive environment, prioritising professional delivery and stakeholder protection is not only a strategic necessity but also a testament to responsible and effective shopping centre management.

Professional Project Delivery in Shopping Centre Management

Professional project delivery in shopping centre management is vital to seamlessly executing a wide array of initiatives, such as renovations, expansions, tenant fit-outs, and promotional events. With meticulous planning, adherence to timelines, and efficient resource allocation, shopping centre managers can ensure that projects are completed on schedule and within budget.

A professionally managed project minimises disruptions to tenants and shoppers, creating a positive experience that encourages footfall and boosts tenant satisfaction. Moreover, it enables shopping centres to stay ahead in a highly competitive retail landscape, attracting new retailers, and enhancing the overall attractiveness of the space to customers.

Advantages of Stakeholder Protection in Shopping Centre Management

Stakeholder protection in shopping centre management entails addressing the concerns and interests of various stakeholders involved in or affected by the shopping centre's operations.

For retailers, this involves providing a conducive business environment, fair lease agreements, and effective marketing support to drive foot traffic. Satisfied retailers are more likely to remain as tenants, reducing vacancies and contributing to a thriving retail ecosystem. Additionally, meeting the expectations of customers by offering a safe, enjoyable, and convenient shopping experience fosters customer loyalty and drives repeat visits.

Investors also benefit from stakeholder protection as they seek to invest in shopping centres with a track record of responsible management and sustained profitability.

Protecting the interests of employees ensures a motivated and engaged workforce, translating into higher productivity and superior customer service.

Furthermore, **taking into account the concerns of the surrounding community, such as traffic management, environmental sustainability, and social responsibility, demonstrates a shopping centre's commitment to being a good corporate citizen. It builds positive community relations and mitigates potential opposition to future expansion plans.**

Some of the salient features from above are discussed below, which highlight the project management deliverables in terms of shopping centre management.

Construction

Introduction

A. Project Overview

1. **Project Name and Location:** The project name refers to the official title of the shopping centre development, while the location indicates the specific geographical site where the project will be constructed. This information provides a clear identification of the development.

2. **Project Scope and Objectives:** The project scope defines the boundaries and deliverables of the shopping centre development. It outlines the key features, facilities, and amenities that the project aims to include. The objectives highlight the goals and purposes of the shopping centre, such as providing a modern retail destination, enhancing the local economy, and creating a vibrant community hub.

B. Project Team and Stakeholders:

1. **Owners and Developers:** The owners and developers are the individuals or organisations responsible for initiating and financing the shopping centre project. They hold the overall vision for the development and have the final decision-making authority.

2. **Project Management Team:** The project management team consists of professionals responsible for overseeing the entire development process. This team ensures efficient project execution, adherence to timelines, budget management, and coordination among various stakeholders.

3. **Architects and Design Consultants:** Architects and design consultants are instrumental in translating the project vision into practical designs. They create detailed floor plans, layouts, and aesthetics that align with the project's goals while also complying with building codes and regulations.

4. **Construction Contractors:** Construction contractors are responsible for executing the actual construction work. They manage the workforce, procure materials, and ensure that construction is carried out according to the approved plans and specifications.

5. **Subcontractors and Vendors:** Subcontractors and vendors are specialised professionals or companies hired by the main construction contractor to handle specific aspects of the project. This may include MEP (Mechanical, Electrical, and Plumbing) works, interior fit-outs, landscaping, and other specialised tasks.

C. **Regulatory and Legal Requirements:**

1. **Building Permits and Approvals:** Obtaining building permits and approvals from local authorities is crucial before commencing construction. These permits ensure that the shopping centre development complies with all safety, zoning, and building regulations set by the governing authorities.

2. **Environmental Compliance:** Shopping centre developments must adhere to environmental regulations to minimise their impact on the surrounding environment. This may involve conducting environmental assessments, implementing sustainable building practices, and ensuring proper waste management.

3. **Zoning and Land Use Regulations:** Zoning and land use regulations govern how land can be used and what types of developments are permitted in specific areas. Compliance with these regulations ensures that the shopping centre aligns with the intended land use and does not violate any zoning restrictions.

D. Project Planning and Design

1. **Site Analysis and Selection**: Site analysis is a critical step in the shopping centre development process, involving a comprehensive evaluation of potential locations to determine the most suitable site for the project. This analysis considers factors such as accessibility, visibility, proximity to transportation hubs, demographics of the surrounding population, competition in the area, and potential for future growth. The goal is to identify a site that aligns with the project's objectives and has the potential to attract the target market.

2. **Conceptual Design and Vision:**

    During the conceptual design phase, the project team collaborates to establish the overall vision and theme of the shopping centre. This includes defining the desired tenant mix, ambiance, architectural style, and overall experience that the centre aims to offer to visitors. The conceptual design lays the foundation for the project's identity and serves as a guide for subsequent design and development stages.

3. **Detailed Design and Layout:**

    The detailed design and layout phase involves transforming the conceptual ideas into tangible plans and blueprints. Architects and design consultants create detailed floor plans, elevations, and 3D renderings that showcase the layout of the shopping centre, including anchor stores, retail spaces, common areas, amenities, parking facilities, and landscaping. Additionally, this phase addresses the integration of MEP (Mechanical, Electrical, and Plumbing) systems to ensure efficient functionality and sustainability of the building.

    The detailed design also encompasses considerations for traffic flow, accessibility compliance, fire safety measures, energy-efficient lighting, and other crucial aspects that contribute to the success of the shopping centre. Throughout this phase, collaboration with stakeholders, tenants, and local authorities is essential to ensure the design aligns with all requirements and preferences.

C.1 Detailed Design and Layout:

1. **Floor Plans**: Floor plans are detailed architectural drawings that illustrate the layout of each level of the shopping centre. They showcase the spatial arrangement of retail stores, common areas, entrances, exits, restrooms, and other amenities. Floor plans help visualise the flow of foot traffic and ensure efficient space utilisation.

2. **Elevations and Façade**: Elevations are drawings that showcase the external appearance of the shopping centre from different viewpoints. They display the building's height, shape, and exterior design elements. Façade refers to the front-facing exterior of the shopping centre, including the entrance, windows, and architectural features. The elevations and façade provide an overall impression of the building's aesthetics.

3. **MEP Systems Layout**: MEP (Mechanical, Electrical, and Plumbing) systems layout comprises detailed plans for the building's infrastructure. It includes the positioning of heating, ventilation, and air conditioning (HVAC) systems, electrical wiring, lighting fixtures, plumbing lines, and fire protection systems. These layouts ensure that the shopping centre functions effectively and safely.

E. Procurement and Bidding Process:

1. **Bid Package Development**: The bid package includes all the necessary documents and information required by contractors to submit their bids for the construction work. It contains project specifications, detailed scope of work, project schedule, contract terms, and any other relevant data. Bid package development ensures that all bidders receive consistent and comprehensive information.

2. **Bid Evaluation Criteria**: Bid evaluation criteria are the standards used to assess and compare bids from different contractors. These criteria

may include factors such as the contractor's experience, financial stability, past performance, proposed schedule, technical capabilities, and compliance with project requirements.

3. **Contractor Selection:** The contractor selection process involves evaluating the submitted bids and choosing the most suitable contractor for the project. The selection is based on the bid evaluation criteria, and the chosen contractor is typically the one offering the best value, expertise, and capability to execute the project successfully.

Pre-Construction Phase

A. **Project Management and Coordination**

1. **Project Manager's Responsibilities:** The Project Manager plays a crucial role in overseeing the entire shopping centre construction project. Their responsibilities include planning, organising, and managing all aspects of the development, from initial concept to completion. They act as the main point of contact for stakeholders, coordinate various teams, ensure adherence to timelines and budgets, and resolve any issues that may arise during the pre-construction phase.

2. **Construction Schedule Development:** During this stage, the project manager, in collaboration with the project team, develops a detailed construction schedule. The schedule outlines the sequence of activities, tasks, and milestones required to complete the shopping centre. It serves as a roadmap for the entire construction process, allowing for effective coordination and timely delivery.

3. **Stakeholder Meetings and Communication:** Effective communication is essential during the pre-construction phase. The project manager conducts regular meetings with stakeholders, including owners, developers, architects, designers, and other relevant parties.

    These meetings provide updates on project progress, address concerns, gather feedback, and ensure alignment with project objectives.

B. **Site preparation and Mobilisation**

1. **Clearing and Grading:** Before construction can begin, the construction site undergoes clearing and grading. This involves removing any existing structures, vegetation, or obstacles from the site to prepare a clean and level surface for construction.

2. **Temporary Facilities Setup:** Temporary facilities, such as site offices, construction trailers, and storage areas, are set up on-site during the pre-construction phase. These facilities serve as command centres for project management and provide a conducive environment for coordination and decision-making.

3. **Site Safety and Security Measures:** Safety is a top priority during construction. The project manager, along with the construction team, implements safety protocols and measures to ensure a secure work environment. This includes safety training for workers, the installation of safety barriers, and compliance with safety regulations.

C. **Building Foundation and Structure**

1. **Excavation and Foundation Construction:** Once the site is prepared, excavation work begins to dig trenches and create the foundation for the shopping centre. The foundation is crucial as it provides the structural support for the entire building. Various foundation types, such as shallow foundations or deep foundations, may be employed based on the site's soil conditions and the building's design.

2. **Structural Framing and Concrete Work:** With the foundation in place, the structural framing and concrete work commence. Structural components, such as columns, beams, and load-bearing walls, are erected according to the architectural and engineering plans. Reinforced concrete is commonly used in construction for its strength and durability.

M. Nauman Thakur

MEP and Civil Works

A. Mechanical, Electrical, and Plumbing (MEP) Installations

   1. **HVAC Systems**: HVAC (Heating, Ventilation, and Air Conditioning) systems are responsible for maintaining a comfortable and controlled indoor environment within the shopping centre. This includes heating and cooling systems, ventilation to ensure air circulation and air conditioning to regulate temperature and humidity levels.

   2. **Electrical Wiring and Lighting**: The electrical installations encompass wiring, distribution boards, switches, and outlets throughout the shopping centre. Adequate lighting is essential for creating a welcoming atmosphere and ensuring visibility for customers and tenants.

   3. **Plumbing and Sanitary Systems**: Plumbing installations consist of water supply networks, drainage systems, and sanitary fixtures like toilets and sinks. These systems are critical for providing water to various areas of the shopping centre and managing wastewater disposal.

B. Fire and Life Safety Systems

   1. **Fire Suppression and Detection**: Fire safety is paramount in any building, and shopping centres are no exception. Fire suppression systems, such as sprinklers and fire extinguishers, are installed to swiftly control and extinguish fires. Additionally, fire detection systems, such as smoke detectors and alarms, provide early warning in case of emergencies.

   2. **Emergency Evacuation Routes**: The shopping centre must have clearly marked emergency evacuation routes and exit signs to guide occupants to safety in the event of a fire or other emergency. These routes are strategically planned and communicated to ensure the swift and orderly evacuation of people.

C. **Infrastructure and Utilities**

   1. **Utility Connections:** Utility connections involve linking the shopping centre to essential services such as electricity, water supply, and gas. These connections are crucial for the functioning of the building and its amenities.

   2. **Drainage and Sewer Systems:** Proper drainage and sewer systems are installed to manage rainwater and wastewater efficiently. Adequate drainage prevents waterlogging and ensures the safety and convenience of shoppers and tenants.

Construction Phase

The construction phase is the actual building process of the shopping centre. It involves the execution of the plans and designs prepared during the pre-construction phase. During this stage:

A. **Progress Monitoring and Quality Control**

   1. **On-Site Inspections and Reports:** During the construction phase, regular on-site inspections are conducted by the Project Manager and relevant stakeholders to assess the progress of the work. These inspections ensure that construction activities align with the approved plans, specifications, and timelines. Inspection reports document the findings, noting any deviations, issues, or areas of improvement.

   2. **Materials Testing and Certifications:** Construction materials used in the shopping centre are subjected to testing and certification processes to ensure they meet industry standards and project requirements. Materials testing includes assessments of strength, durability, fire resistance, and other critical properties. Certifications provide evidence of compliance and quality assurance.

B. Construction Safety and Compliance

   1. **Occupational Health and Safety Measures:** Safety is of paramount importance during the construction phase. Occupational health and safety measures are implemented to protect workers and mitigate potential hazards. Personal protective equipment (PPE), safety protocols, and training programs are enforced to create a secure working environment.

   2. **Compliance with Building Codes and Standards:** The construction phase involves strict adherence to building codes, regulations, and industry standards. Compliance ensures that the shopping centre meets all legal requirements and safety norms, guaranteeing the well-being of occupants and visitors.

C. Tenant Coordination and Fit-Outs

   1. **Tenants' Responsibilities and Guidelines:** During the construction phase, tenants are provided with guidelines and responsibilities for their fit-out works. This includes specifications for structural modifications, electrical connections, and design standards to maintain uniformity and safety within their leased spaces.

   2. **Inspections of Completed Tenant Spaces:** After the tenants complete their fit-out works, inspections are carried out to verify that the construction aligns with the approved plans and follows all regulations. This process ensures that the tenants' spaces are ready for operation and meet the necessary standards.

Project Completion and Handover

A. Defect Liability Period

   1. **Identification and Documentation of Defects:** The Defect Liability Period commences after substantial completion of the shopping centre.

During this period, typically ranging from six months to one year, any defects or issues found in the construction are documented. The project manager, along with relevant consultants and stakeholders, conducts thorough inspections to identify and record these defects.

2. **Rectification and Repair Procedures**: Once defects are identified, the construction team is responsible for rectification and repairs. The contractor addresses and resolves the documented issues within the Defect Liability Period at no additional cost to the owner. The goal is to ensure that the shopping centre achieves the desired quality standards.

The successful completion of the construction phase sets the stage for the subsequent stages, including tenant fit-out, testing, commissioning, and ultimately, the grand opening of the shopping centre.

B. **Testing and Commissioning**

1. **MEP Systems Testing**: MEP systems (Mechanical, Electrical, and Plumbing) undergo rigorous testing to ensure their proper functioning and adherence to design specifications. This includes testing HVAC systems to verify heating, cooling, and ventilation performance; electrical systems for safety and efficiency; and plumbing systems to check water supply, drainage, and sanitation. Testing ensures that all MEP components work seamlessly together, contributing to the overall functionality and comfort of the shopping centre.

2. **Fire and Life Safety Testing**: Fire and life safety systems are subject to comprehensive testing to assess their reliability and effectiveness in emergencies. This involves testing fire suppression and detection systems, emergency lighting, fire alarms, and evacuation routes. The goal is to ensure that the shopping centre is well-equipped to handle fire incidents and safely evacuate occupants if necessary.

3. **Elevator and Escalator Testing**: Elevators and escalators are critical elements of a shopping centre's vertical transportation system. Testing involves examining their mechanical and electrical components,

emergency features, and smooth operation. Properly functioning elevators and escalators are vital for providing easy access to various levels of the shopping centre.

Examples of MEP (Mechanical, Electrical, and Plumbing) Equipment:

1. HVAC (Heating, Ventilation, and Air Conditioning) Systems:

   - Chillers
   - Air Handling Units (AHUs)
   - Cooling Towers
   - Fan Coil Units (FCUs)
   - VRF (Variable Refrigerant Flow) Systems
   - Ductwork and Diffusers
   - Thermostats and Temperature Sensors

2. Electrical Systems:

   - Transformers
   - Switchgear and Distribution Panels
   - Circuit Breakers
   - Electrical Wiring and Cables
   - Lighting Fixtures (LED, Fluorescent, etc.)
   - Emergency Lighting and Exit Signs
   - Electrical Outlets and Receptacles
   - Electrical Metres and Sub-Meters

3. Plumbing and Sanitary Systems:

- Water Supply Pipes and Valves
- Water Heaters and Boilers
- Water Pumps
- Drainage Pipes and Fittings
- Sanitary Fixtures (Toilets, Sinks, etc.)
- Water Metres
- Grease Traps

Checklist for MEP Testing and Commissioning

1. HVAC Systems Testing and Commissioning:

- Verification of HVAC system installation against design drawings and specifications.
- Functional testing of chillers, AHUs, FCUs, and VRF systems to ensure proper operation and performance.
- Testing and balancing of air and water distribution systems to achieve design flow rates and temperatures.
- Calibration of thermostats and temperature sensors for accurate control.
- Assessment of ventilation rates to comply with indoor air quality standards.

2. Electrical Systems Testing and Commissioning:

- Verification of electrical system installation, including wiring, distribution panels, and electrical equipment.

- Testing of transformers and switchgear for proper functioning and load capacity.

- Circuit testing to ensure proper connectivity and no electrical faults.

- Functional testing of lighting fixtures and emergency lighting systems.

- Measurement of electrical consumption using metres and sub-meters.

3. **Plumbing and Sanitary Systems Testing and Commissioning:**

   - Inspection of water supply pipes and valves for leaks and proper flow rates.

   - Testing of water heaters and boilers for correct operation and temperature control.

   - Performance testing of water pumps for adequate water pressure.

   - Verification of proper drainage flow and functionality of sanitary fixtures.

   - Measurement of water consumption using water metres.

4. **Fire and Life Safety Systems Testing and Commissioning:**

   - Testing of fire detection systems, including smoke detectors and fire alarms.

   - Verification of the operation of fire suppression systems such as sprinklers and fire extinguishers.

   - Testing of emergency lighting and exit signs for functionality during power outages.

   - Simulation of emergency evacuation procedures and routes.

5. **Elevator and Escalator Testing and Commissioning:**

    - Functional testing of elevators and escalators for smooth operation and safety features.

    - Load testing to ensure elevators can handle their rated capacity.

    - Inspection of emergency communication systems within elevators.

6. **Other MEP Systems Testing and Commissioning:**

    - Testing of security systems, including CCTV cameras and access control devices.

    - Verification of communication systems, such as telephone and data networks.

The checklist should include detailed procedures for each test, specific parameters to be measured, acceptable performance thresholds, and documentation requirements. Regular inspections, functional tests, and performance evaluations are crucial to ensure that MEP systems are operating efficiently, meeting safety standards, and providing a comfortable environment for occupants. Any deviations or deficiencies found during testing and commissioning should be addressed and rectified promptly to ensuring the shopping centre's smooth and safe operation.

C. **Final Inspection and Certificate of Occupancy**

   1. **Building Inspections and Approvals:** Before obtaining the Certificate of Occupancy, the shopping centre undergoes a final inspection by relevant authorities. Inspectors review the building's compliance with construction codes, safety regulations, and design specifications. Once the shopping centre meets all requirements, it is eligible to receive the Certificate of Occupancy, allowing for legal occupancy and operation.

   2. **Compliance with Regulations:** The final inspection process ensures that the shopping centre fully complies with all relevant regulatory and legal

requirements. This includes adherence to building codes, environmental regulations, zoning ordinances, and accessibility standards. Compliance is crucial to ensure the safety and well-being of occupants and visitors.

D. Handover and Occupancy

1. **Handover of Common Areas and Tenant Spaces**: Upon receiving the necessary approvals and certificates, the construction team formally hands over the completed shopping centre to the property management team or owners. The handover includes the common areas such as lobbies, corridors, and shared facilities, as well as individual tenant spaces. A comprehensive handover document is prepared, detailing the condition of each area and confirming that all contractual obligations have been fulfilled.

2. **Tenant Opening and Operations:**

   After the handover, tenants are granted access to their respective spaces to commence their fit-out works. Each tenant is responsible for setting up their stores according to the approved designs and complying with the shopping centre's rules and regulations. The property management team coordinates with tenants during this process to ensure a smooth transition to the operational phase.

Post-Construction Stage

A. Facility and Asset Management

1. **Facility Maintenance and Upkeep**: Facility management involves the ongoing maintenance and upkeep of the shopping centre's physical assets. Regular inspections and preventive maintenance are performed on building systems, equipment, and common areas to ensure their proper functioning and longevity. Any repairs or replacements needed are promptly addressed to maintain the shopping centre's operational efficiency.

2. **Asset Inventory and Documentation**: Asset management entails maintaining a comprehensive inventory of all assets within the shopping

centre, including equipment, furniture, fixtures, and other movable property. Documentation of assets, their condition, and service history is essential for effective maintenance, financial planning, and reporting.

B. **Operations and Tenant Relations**

1. **Ongoing Property Management:** The property management team oversees the day-to-day operations of the shopping centre. This includes tenant relations, lease management, rent collection, security, housekeeping, and ensuring a pleasant shopping experience for visitors. They address any tenant concerns, manage service contracts, and handle general administrative tasks.

2. **Lease Renewals and Tenant Support:** During the post-construction stage, the property management team handles lease renewals with existing tenants. They also provide ongoing support to tenants, addressing any issues they may encounter and assisting in resolving operational challenges.

C. **Marketing and Promotion**

1. **Marketing Initiatives and Events:** To attract visitors and maintain footfall, marketing initiatives and events are organised regularly. These may include seasonal sales, promotional campaigns, special events, and partnerships with brands or community organisations. Marketing efforts aim to enhance the shopping centre's visibility and increase customer engagement.

2. **Tenant Promotions and Collaborations**: Collaboration with tenants on marketing and promotional activities is encouraged to create a unified and vibrant shopping environment. Joint promotions, discounts, and loyalty programmes involving multiple tenants can boost customer interest and loyalty.

- The post-construction stage focuses on maintaining the shopping centre's operational efficiency, providing excellent tenant support, ensuring a safe and enjoyable shopping experience for visitors, and actively marketing the centre to attract a diverse and engaged customer base.

HVAC Testing and Commissioning Checklist

1. **Chiller System**

   - Verify installation of chillers as per manufacturer's guidelines.
   - Check chiller controls for proper operation.
   - Conduct performance testing to ensure cooling capacity.
   - Inspect refrigerant levels and connections.

2. **Air Handling Units (AHUs)**

   - Check AHU installation and alignment.
   - Test AHU fan operation and airflow.
   - Verify damper control and positioning.
   - Measure and adjust discharge air temperatures.

3. **Ventilation and Air Distribution**

   - Conduct air balancing and adjust registers as needed.
   - Check ventilation rates and air changes per hour.
   - Verify the operation of exhaust fans and dampers.
   - Inspect air filters and replace them as necessary.

4. Temperature and Humidity Control

  - Calibrate thermostats and sensors.
  - Verify temperature and humidity setpoints.
  - Check for temperature stratification issues.

Electrical Systems Testing and Commissioning Checklist

1. Switchgear and Distribution Panels

  - Verify proper installation and connections.
  - Conduct insulation resistance and continuity testing.
  - Check circuit breaker operations and settings.

2. Lighting Systems

  - Test all lighting fixtures for proper illumination.
  - Verify functionality of emergency lighting and exit signs.
  - Measure lighting levels in different areas.

3. Electrical Outlets

  - Test electrical outlets for power supply.
  - Verify grounding and polarity.

4. Electrical Metres

  - Check the accuracy of electrical metres.
  - Verify metre readings with actual consumption.

Plumbing and Sanitary Systems Testing and Commissioning Checklist

1. Water Supply and Distribution

   - Verify water supply connections and flow rates.

   - Check for leaks in pipes and fittings.

   - Test water pressure at various points.

2. Water Heaters and Boilers

   - Check temperature control and safety features.

   - Verify proper venting and exhaust systems.

3. Sanitary Fixtures

   - Test functionality of toilets, sinks, and faucets.

   - Check drainage flow and identify any blockages.

4. Water Metres

   - Verify the accuracy of water metres.

   - Compare metre readings with actual consumption.

Fire and Life Safety Systems Testing and Commissioning Checklist

1. Fire Detection and Alarm Systems

   - Test smoke detectors and heat sensors.

   - Verify the functionality of fire alarm panels.

- Conduct sound testing of fire alarms.

2. **Fire Suppression Systems**

    - Test sprinkler systems for proper coverage and activation.

    - Verify the operation of fire extinguishers and hose reels.

3. **Emergency Evacuation Routes**

    - Conduct emergency evacuation drills.

    - Verify signage and visibility of evacuation routes.

Elevator and Escalator Testing and Commissioning Checklist

1. **Elevators**

    - Test elevator operation and controls.

    - Verify safety features and emergency communication.

2. **Escalators**

    - Check escalator operation and speed.

    - Verify safety sensors and emergency stop function.

Above are the checklist examples of the MEP Testing and Commissioning of the equipment's and safeguards all the requirements as per the specifications of the stakeholders prior operation and functioning of the shopping centre.

Defect Liability Period

Defect Liability Period (DLP), also known as the warranty period or maintenance period, is a critical phase that comes into play after the completion of a construction project, including shopping centres. During this period, the contractor or construction company is responsible for rectifying any defects or issues that arise in the completed work. The DLP is usually specified in the construction contract and typically ranges from 6 months to 1 year, depending on the terms negotiated between the parties.

Purpose of the Defect Liability Period:

The primary purpose of the Defect Liability Period is to ensure that the construction work meets the required quality standards and is free from any defects or deficiencies. It provides a buffer for the client or owner to identify and report any issues that may arise during the initial occupancy and use of the shopping centre. The contractor, during this period, is obligated to fix or rectify these defects at no additional cost to the client.

Defect Liability Protocol

The Defect Liability Protocol is a formal procedure that outlines the roles, responsibilities, and processes involved during the Defect Liability Period. It serves as a guideline for both the client and the contractor to manage the rectification of defects efficiently.

Below are the key components of a typical Defect Liability Protocol:

1. **Defect Identification:** The client or their representatives, such as the shopping centre manager or facility management team, conduct regular inspections during the Defect Liability Period to identify any defects or issues. Defects can range from structural problems to non-functional equipment or finishing defects.

2. **Reporting Process:** Once a defect is identified, the client submits a formal defect report to the contractor, providing clear and detailed information about the issue, its location, and any other relevant details. This report initiates the process of rectification.

3. **Response Time:** The Defect Liability Protocol specifies a response time within which the contractor must acknowledge receipt of the defect report and schedule an inspection to verify the reported issue.

4. **Inspection and Verification:** The contractor inspects and verifies the reported defects to ensure that they are genuine and fall under their responsibility. If the issue is valid, they proceed with the rectification process.

5. **Rectification Process:** The contractor is required to rectify the reported defects promptly and professionally. The protocol may include specific timelines for rectification based on the severity of the defects.

6. **Quality Assurance:** After rectification, the contractor may need to provide documentation or evidence that the issues have been resolved satisfactorily. The client or their representatives conduct follow-up inspections to confirm the completion of rectification.

7. **Final Inspection and Sign-off:** Towards the end of the Defect Liability Period, a final inspection is conducted to ensure that all reported defects have been rectified. If everything meets the required standards, the client issues a formal sign-off, indicating the successful completion of the Defect Liability Period.

Mitigating Delays and Protecting Stakeholders' Equity

1. **Contractual Agreements and Penalty Clauses:** The importance of clear and comprehensive contractual agreements cannot be overstated. The contract between the main contractor and the stakeholders should include well-defined timelines and milestones for construction and handover. Penalty clauses can be incorporated to incentivise the contractor to adhere to the schedule. These penalties could involve financial deductions for each day of delay beyond the agreed-upon completion date.

2. **Performance Bonds and Guarantees:** To provide additional security and assurance, the main contractor can be required to post a performance bond or provide guarantees. Performance bonds act as a form of insurance that compensates the stakeholders if the contractor fails to meet their obligations. This helps protect the ownership from financial losses caused by delays.

3. **Liquidated Damages:** Liquidated damages clauses specify a predetermined amount that the main contractor will be liable to pay for each day of delay. This amount is agreed upon and documented in the contract. Liquidated damages can serve as a fair and predetermined measure of compensation for the stakeholders if the project completion date is not met.

4. **Early Warning System:** Implementing an early warning system allows the project management team to identify potential delays in advance. By closely monitoring project progress and identifying issues early on, stakeholders can take corrective measures or activate contingency plans to minimise the impact of delays.

5. **Contingency Planning:** The risk management document should include well-defined contingency plans to address potential delays. These plans outline alternative courses of action that can be taken if delays occur, such as engaging backup contractors or reallocating resources.

6. **Open Communication and Negotiation:** It is crucial to maintain open lines of communication with the main contractor throughout the project. If delays arise, stakeholders should engage in constructive negotiations to understand the reasons for the delay and explore potential solutions.

7. **Performance Reviews and Audits:** Regular performance reviews and audits of the main contractor's activities can help ensure compliance with the agreed-upon schedule and quality standards. These reviews can identify any early signs of potential delays and allow stakeholders to take appropriate actions.

8. **Dispute Resolution Mechanism:** The contract should include a clearly defined dispute resolution mechanism to handle disagreements or conflicts that may arise due to delays. This mechanism can facilitate prompt resolution and avoid protracted legal disputes.

This essential document instrumentation safeguards the interests of the stakeholder, minimises the impact of delays, protects their financial interests, and ensures a successful shopping centre construction and handover process. These measures create a framework of accountability and incentivise the main contractor to meet their commitments, reducing the risk of financial losses and liabilities for the ownership.

Conclusion: In the realm of shopping centre management, professional project delivery and stakeholder protection are indispensable elements for long-term success. By efficiently executing projects and prioritising the well-being of tenants, customers, investors, employees, and the community, shopping centres can create an environment that attracts and retains stakeholders while sustaining a competitive advantage. Embracing these principles not only ensures the growth and profitability of shopping centres but also fosters trust, loyalty, and a positive impact on the community they serve.

Introduction To Shopping Centre Operational Metrics

Shopping Centre Operational Metrics are quantitative measures used to assess the performance and effectiveness of a shopping centre's operations. These metrics play a crucial role in tracking and evaluating key aspects of the shopping centre's operations, enabling informed decisions and driving improvements.

Key Shopping Centre Operational Metrics

A. **Sales Metrics Sales per Square Foot:**

Sales per square foot measure the revenue generated per unit of space in the shopping centre. It provides insights into the shopping centre's productivity, profitability, and the effectiveness of tenant mix and merchandising strategies. A higher sales per square foot indicates better financial performance and efficient utilisation of the shopping centre's space

- Tenant Sales Growth: Tenant sales growth measures the year-on-year revenue growth of individual tenants within the shopping centre. This metric helps identify successful tenants, monitor their performance, and assess the impact of tenant mix on overall sales growth. Understanding tenant sales growth assists in optimising the tenant mix and identifying opportunities for enhancing the shopping centre's revenue potential.

B. **Occupancy Metrics**

Occupancy Rate: The occupancy rate represents the percentage of leasable space that is currently occupied by tenants. It reflects the shopping centre's attractiveness to tenants and indicates the success of leasing efforts. A higher occupancy rate signifies higher demand for space and potential for rental income. Monitoring the occupancy rate is essential for shopping centre operators, as it provides valuable insights into the leasing performance and the overall health of the centre.

Benefits of Tracking Occupancy Rate

- **Assurance to Tenants:**

A high occupancy rate indicates that the shopping centre is appealing to tenants, as it demonstrates a thriving business environment. Prospective tenants are more likely to be interested in leasing space in a shopping centre with a high occupancy rate, as it signifies a vibrant and active customer base.

- **Rental Income Generation:**

Occupancy rate directly impacts the shopping centre's financial performance. A higher occupancy rate means more tenants are occupying the space, resulting in increased rental income. This revenue contributes to the profitability and sustainability of the shopping centre.

- **Tenant Mix Evaluation:**

By monitoring occupancy rates, shopping centre operators can assess the effectiveness of their tenant mix. A well-balanced and diverse tenant mix can attract a wider customer base and drive footfall, resulting in higher occupancy rates. Analysing occupancy rates for different categories of tenants can help identify potential gaps or opportunities in the tenant mix and inform leasing decisions.

- **Lease Renewals and Negotiations:**

Occupancy rate data is crucial during lease renewal negotiations. It provides bargaining power for the shopping centre operator, especially if the occupancy rate is high, indicating a high demand for space. Operators can use this data to negotiate favourable terms with existing tenants, ensuring the continued occupancy and stability of the centre.

- **Benchmarking and Competitiveness:**

  The occupancy rate serves as a benchmark for comparing the shopping centre's performance against industry standards and competitors. A higher occupancy rate than the industry average signifies a stronger position in the market and enhances the shopping centre's competitiveness.

- **Identifying Underperforming Areas:**

  Monitoring occupancy rates can help identify underperforming areas within the shopping centre. If certain sections or floors consistently show low occupancy rates, it may indicate a need for strategic interventions, such as targeted marketing campaigns or lease renegotiations, to attract new tenants and improve overall occupancy rates.

- **Planning and Expansion:**

  Occupancy rate data is crucial for future planning and expansion initiatives. By analysing historical occupancy trends and projected demand, shopping centre operators can make informed decisions regarding expansion plans, determining the feasibility and potential profitability of new developments. Monitoring the occupancy rate is vital for shopping centre operators to assess leasing performance, attract tenants, generate rental income, and ensure the overall success of the centre.

  It determines the health of the shopping centre, and the effectiveness of the tenant mix, and serves as a benchmark for industry comparison. By actively managing and optimising occupancy rates, operators can enhance the financial performance and long-term sustainability of the shopping centre.

C. **Footfall and Traffic Metrics**

  Footfall or Traffic Count: Footfall or traffic count measures the number of visitors entering the shopping centre over a specific period. This metric provides insights into the shopping centre's popularity and can be used to evaluate the effectiveness of marketing campaigns, identify peak hours, and optimise tenant placement. By tracking footfall, shopping centre operators can better understand visitor trends and adjust operations accordingly to enhance the overall customer experience.

D. **Customer Behaviour Metrics**

I. **Average Transaction Value:**

Average transaction value calculates the average amount spent by customers per transaction. This metric helps assess the effectiveness of pricing strategies, promotional campaigns, and upselling efforts. By analysing the average transaction value, shopping centre operators can identify opportunities to increase customer spending, optimise pricing strategies, and enhance revenue generation.

Using Shopping Centre Operational Metrics

- **Performance Monitoring:**

  Shopping centre operational metrics enable ongoing monitoring of performance, providing insights into the shopping centre's overall health and identifying areas that require attention or improvement. By regularly tracking and analysing these metrics, operators can proactively address issues and optimise operations.

- **Decision Making:**

  Shopping centre operational metrics serve as a basis for data-driven decision-making. They guide strategic choices related to leasing, tenant mix, marketing campaigns, facility management, and overall operations. By relying on concrete data and insights from operational metrics, operators can make informed decisions that align with the shopping centre's goals and objectives.

- **Benchmarking and Comparison:**

  Operational metrics facilitate benchmarking against industry standards and competitors. By comparing performance metrics with those of similar shopping centres, operators can identify areas of strength and areas needing improvement. This enables a proactive approach to stay competitive and drive continuous improvement.

- **Performance Incentives:**

Operational metrics can be used to establish performance-based incentives for tenants. By incentivising tenants based on metrics such as sales growth or customer satisfaction, shopping centre operators can motivate them to improve their performance and contribute to the shopping centre's success. This creates a win-win situation where both the shopping centre and its tenants benefit from improved performance.

- **Reporting and Communication:**

Shopping centre operational metrics provide a standardised language for reporting performance to stakeholders, including owners, investors, tenants, and management. By regularly sharing metrics-based reports and analyses, operators can ensure transparent communication, demonstrate accountability, and align stakeholders towards shared goals.

Challenges and Considerations

Data Accuracy and Availability: Ensuring accurate and timely data collection can be challenging, as it may involve gathering information from various sources. Establishing robust systems and processes for data collection and validation is crucial to ensure data accuracy and availability.

- **Contextual Analysis:**

Metrics should be analysed in conjunction with qualitative insights and market trends to provide a comprehensive understanding of performance. While metrics provide quantitative data, contextual analysis helps interpret the metrics and uncover underlying factors that contribute to performance trends.

- **Evolving Metrics:**

    As the shopping centre industry evolves, new metrics may emerge to capture changing dynamics and consumer behaviours. It is essential for shopping centre operators to regularly review and update their metrics to ensure relevance and alignment with industry trends and best practices.

Key Takeaways

Shopping centre operational metrics play a vital role in assessing and optimising the performance of shopping centres. By tracking and analysing these metrics, management can make data-driven decisions, improve operations, and enhance the overall shopping experience for customers and tenants. These metrics provide valuable insights into various aspects of a shopping centre's operations, enabling operators to identify areas of strength, address areas for improvement, and drive sustainable growth and success.

QUESTIONS AND ANSWERS SESSION - METRICS

Q1: **How do sales metrics contribute to the evaluation of a shopping centre's performance?**

A1: Sales metrics provide insights into the financial performance of a shopping centre by measuring factors such as total sales revenue, average transaction value, sales per square foot, and sales growth.

Q2: **What are occupancy metrics, and why are they important for shopping centres?**

A2: Occupancy metrics measure the percentage of leasable space that is currently occupied by tenants. These metrics help assess the leasing health of a shopping centre, monitor tenant turnover, and determine the overall attractiveness of the shopping centre to potential tenants.

Glossary

HSE and Its Practices

1. Risk Assessment Management: The process of identifying potential hazards, evaluating risks, and implementing measures to mitigate and manage health, safety, and environmental risks within the shopping centre.

2. Emergency Management: Preparedness and response procedures to handle crises and emergencies, such as fires, natural disasters, or security threats, to protect visitors, tenants, and assets.

Shopping Centre Metrics

1. Footfall: The number of visitors or pedestrians entering the shopping centre over a specific period, indicating the level of customer traffic.

2. Customer Behavior Metrics: Data and analysis on customer interactions, preferences, and spending habits, used to enhance the shopping centre's offerings and improve customer satisfaction.

These definitions provide a foundational understanding of key terms and concepts used throughout the handbook, enabling professionals in shopping centre management to navigate the content effectively and make informed decisions.

This Handbook is designed to provide a helpful and informative overview of the topics covered. It is not intended to be a substitute for more extensive learning that can be achieved through attending ICSC educational programs and reading additional ICSC professional publications.

You Write. We Publish.

To publish your own book, contact us.

We publish poetry collections, short story collections, novellas and novels.

contact@thewriteorder.com

Instagram- thewriteorder

www.facebook.com/thewriteorder

www.ingramcontent.com/pod-product-compliance
Lightning Source LLC
LaVergne TN
LVHW091716070526
838199LV00050B/2421